Unfortunately, infertility is a affecting one in eight couples. a particularly long and difficult one. *Life After Infertility* is an essential resource for others facing fertility issues. More importantly, this book is an invaluable guide for friends and family members of couples struggling to conceive. It illustrates how we can more effectively demonstrate God's love and encouragement to those who travel the tough road of infertility.

William G. Dodds, M.D.
Reproductive Endocrinology Specialist
Founder and Director,
The Fertility Center

Life After Infertility eloquently describes one of our deepest longings as humans: to become parents. Sarah tells an authentic, tender story of the journey through infertility, and poignantly describes the uncertainties of the adoption process. She shares the thoughts, feelings, doubts, and frustrations that couples wishing for a baby can surely relate to. Throughout the story, she candidly communicates her vulnerability—you will laugh one minute, and have tears in your eyes the next. The story leaves the reader with no doubt that God has a plan for his children and that each new person who enters the world is a miraculous, precious gift. *Life After Infertility* is a must-read for anyone wanting to more deeply and meaningfully understand that parenthood sometimes, finally, comes in ways you may not have planned for, but are profoundly blessed by nonetheless.

Michelle Dykema, LMSW
Executive Director,
Adoption Associates, Inc.

LIFE AFTER

Infertility

A Story of Hope
for Those Who Wait

SARAH SISSON ROLLANDINI

ISBN: 978-0-578-67534-3

Printed in the United States of America.

Cover Design by 100Covers.com
Interior Design by FormattedBooks.com

DOWNLOAD

THE LIFE AFTER INFERTILITY

E-CALENDAR FREE!

READ THIS FIRST

Just to say "thanks" for buying my book, I would like to give you the
e-calendar, with clickable links to stories, advice,
and encouragement 100% FREE!

TO DOWNLOAD GO TO

Life After Infertility E-Calendar

Angel -
May God's presence
lift you when you
experience hard things
Gird your loins! :)
    In Christ,
    Sarah Sisson
    Rolland

Dedication

This book is dedicated to the loves of my life
Mark, Adelaine, Faith, and Mark Westfield

And to my mom and dad, my biggest cheerleaders
Lorna and Craig Sisson

Of one thing I am perfectly sure: God's story never ends with ashes.

—Elisabeth Elliot

CONTENTS

INTRODUCTION

"Breathe, darling. This is just a chapter.
It's not your whole story."

S.C. Lourie

𝓘nfertility stinks. As you read this, one in eight women is grappling with the fact that her body has failed to live up to her—and society's—expectations. Yes, reproductive technologies have come a long way. And yes, high-profile celebrities such as Khloé Kardashian and Gabrielle Union have come out of the woodwork to share their struggles with achieving pregnancy. However, despite notable progress in treatment and a growing awareness of the problem, women in the midst of TTC (Trying To Conceive) still feel very much alone on their journeys.

Life after Infertility is not a "how-to" book. It does not lay out the latest fertility diet, recommend the most outstanding doctors or tell you how to fix the problem. Instead, this memoir tells a true story of infertility survival. Its aim is to dispel the feeling of isolation that is an inevitable part of the TTC experience.

My husband and I endured 10 seemingly endless years of infertility, including multiple rounds of meds, intrauterine inseminations, and in vitro fertilizations (and all the acronyms that go with it). We also braved miscarriage, tubal pregnancy, probing questions (read: probing doctors!), vacillating birth mothers, one old-school county judge, and plenty of stupid advice. Our infertility experience caused me to question myself, my marriage, and my faith. Every day, I asked one haunting question: *Will I ever have the family I've dreamed of?*

If you feel alone, if you find yourself anxious about the future, ashamed of your (or your husband's) underperforming body, or doubtful that you'll ever reach your happy ending, this book will provide the encouragement you need to persevere.

If you are the mom, sister, cousin, BFF, or co-worker of someone facing infertility, our story will provide you with a context in which to offer true help and comfort.

If you're angry with God and have had it up to your eyeballs with Christian platitudes, this book will spur you to choose daily hope over bitterness.

Above it all, *Life after Infertility* contains the humorous and heart-wrenching stories of a seasoned survivor. It is a narrative that will inspire you to overcome TTC's unexpected challenges with a new sense of courage and determination.

Infertility is just a chapter, darling. Your beautiful story has yet to unfold.

CHAPTER 1

Wishing and Hoping

*M*y husband found me, bent and sobbing, in the middle of the empty room holding a tiny and perfectly new cotton onesie to my chest. Rocking back and forth, I struggled to catch my breath as grief surrounded me like an October fog. The room I had hoped to fill with the smell of lavender and the soft strains of "Amazing Grace" still stood empty…like me.

All the diligent research on infertility interventions and the grueling treatments themselves had boomeranged me to this familiar place—childlessness—and after four years of prayer and positivity, I had reached the end of myself.

At 31 years old, being childless among so many "child-full" people had banished me to an entirely different planet. Before my experience with infertility, life had plugged along according to my plans. College degrees? Check. A career teaching deaf kids? Check. Marriage to soul mate? Check. It was only after I had experienced the earthquake of infertility that I questioned my naïveté. Had I ever controlled my life's course or had I achieved my previous goals thanks to dumb luck? Not that I believe in luck, per se, except to note that I was lucky that my agenda aligned with God's game plan for me until I hit the age of 27. After that came five years in which God and I were on distinctly different pages, and I wrestled with him like a contender in a heavyweight world tournament.

My dreams of having a family with a pack of rambunctious kids went back to a time when I pressed my five-year-old hand into wet cement on the front porch of my new playhouse and assumed the role of Mommy to my dolls and stuffed animals and any neighborhood kids who were willing. I couldn't separate my yearning for children from the rest of me, which led me to believe that if the mothering part of me was left to wither, the rest of me would follow suit. The most difficult lesson in my 27 years came down to one terrifying idea: *I am not in control.* In the end, this truth would free me from a shallow faith that had allowed me to spend a quarter of my life on cruise control.

The Path

My husband, Mark, and I started "Operation Baby" on a celebratory Valentine's weekend getaway. We'd been married for three years and were jumping ahead of our initial plans for starting a family, but only by a few months. Wouldn't making a baby on the holiday that honors love and lovers be a sweet story to tell when we soon announced our pregnancy?

Looking back on our conversation that weekend, I am incredulous at our unbridled optimism. Though I know many couples have followed a similar plan, it seems unjust that pregnancy can be achieved on the meager $50 budget required for a pre-copulation dinner and a movie. Most pregnancies, in fact, require a far smaller budget.

In truth, my trip from glass-half-full to glass-utterly-empty was short. After a few months of trying, I became convinced that the successful joining of egg and sperm was taking way too long to be normal. The obvious explanation: something was amiss with one of the donors.

Despite my concern, I refused to panic. Infertility was a challenge that I could crush as I had all others: by putting my brain to work. After all, I had a graduate degree.

With this plucky outlook, I ordered the book *Resolving Infertility: Understanding the Options and Choosing Solutions When You Want to Have a Baby*. Along with scouring the internet, I devoured every page of this manual, certain it would solve and resolve (look at its title!) our dilemma.

The book did helpfully lay out solutions, and Mark and I traipsed down a rosy path that began with the "just wait and see" approach to conception. This same path meandered into a mess of grueling treatment options that would land most couples either on the crazy train or in the poorhouse. Regardless, I was raring to go. My husband, however, was not so eager.

He was quite content to stay on our current groove of "wait and see" and "I'm perfectly happy with you, my beautiful wife, and growing old with just the two of us would suit me fine." I love him for his devotion. My husband put zero pressure on us to have a baby. His nonchalance counter-balanced my intensity since, for me, having a family was the gold standard for a healthy marriage and a fulfilled life. Mark's clearer (read: saner) per-spective on family planning grounded me, but I dragged him along on this journey toward pregnancy and he supported me with the loyalty of a golden retriever.

I had the path all mapped out, and it followed exactly the approach prescribed in *Resolving Infertility*, which might as well have been the Bible during my drive toward pregnancy. In hindsight, it's possible I could've spent more time reading the *actual* Bible. Fact: Learning to trust and rely on God entails a considerable learning curve.

So, the path. It went like this:

Step 1: Testing
Test husband and wife to find out what the heck is wrong with man/woman/couple.

Step 2: Medication and making love
Take mild infertility drug while trying for three to six months to make a baby the old-fashioned way.

Step 3: Intrauterine Insemination (IUI)
Undergo three to six cycles of IUI, fondly referred to as the "turkey baster method."

Step 4: *In vitro* Fertilization (IVF)

Go through two to three cycles of IVF in various forms (fresh, frozen, zygote intrafollopian transfer—ZIFT, gamete intrafallopian transfer—GIFT) coupled with industrial strength infertility drugs and $12,000–$15,000 price tag per cycle. In IVF, technicians remove a woman's eggs and a man's sperm and introduce them in a blind date in a petri dish. A few days later, specialists place the resulting embryos *in utero* hoping for implantation.

Step 5: Use of donor egg or sperm

If specialists determine the egg or sperm to be shoddy, use donor egg or sperm along with pregnancy-inducing drugs to create a baby and then place the baby in the woman's uterus. The rationale behind this treatment is that if a couple's reproductive cells don't hit it off, introducing a more exciting stranger might get the party started.

Step 6: Use of donor embryo

If introducing donor egg or sperm is a flop, use pregnancy-inducing drugs along with a donor embryo and deposit in the woman's uterus. Sometimes a couple's genetics are incompatible and there are plenty of frozen embryos that have been created through IVF waiting for a womb to call home. In this case, the woman could still be an incubator for said embryo.

Step 7: Use of gestational carrier

Use of a carrier (i.e. another woman) and drug cocktails for two (egg making for bio mom and pregnancy-inducing for carrier). Some people refer to this arrangement as surrogacy, but, technically, a surrogate donates her egg *and* room in her womb. A gestational carrier simply carries a husband and wife's embryo, becoming an incubator for someone else's biological child.

Step 8: Adoption

At age 27, staring down a decade of childbearing potential, reaching Step 8 seemed about as likely as being struck by lightning, thus its position at list's end.

Ah, the path. It was my step-by-step guide for how to make a baby, affording a brief and artificial sense of peace. Surely if I stuck to the list, I would achieve the desired result: a baby, motherhood, a happily ever after. Hard work plus a plan yields success. A + B = C. In all my experiences to date, this logic had worked beautifully, which meant that it must be valid. Only...what if it wasn't?

Testing

Oddly, I looked forward to testing like Martha Stewart looks forward to spring cleaning. It was the first progressive step on the path that would lead to our baby. Never mind that 95% of the testing involved me being poked and prodded in places that—until our foray into infertility treatment— were off limits to all but my lucky husband.

Never mind that the testing involved scheduling, planning, charting, and sharing the minutia of our sex life with a host of nurses, doctors, phlebotomists, ultrasound techs, and the occasional medical student on intern rotation.

Doctor: "Do you mind if our intern, Dr. Young & Attractive, sits in on this trans-vaginal ultrasound?"

Me: "No problem!"

You're welcome, Dr. Young & Attractive, I thought. *You can thank me in your graduation speech.*

Clearly, at 27-years-old, I presumed that my positive, helpful attitude would put me on the fast track to pregnancy; that being a good person, a rule follower, would protect me from experiencing infertility's pain and injustice. Even as a woman who claimed to live by God's grace, I depended on life's fairness.

But Step 1 on the path was no time for spiritual navel-gazing. There was work to be done!

Checking my basal body temperature each morning upon waking, I recorded the reading to the nearest 10th degree on my bedside chart.

My husband begrudgingly presented his semen for analysis—though, come to think of it, what was he begrudging? Just saying.

I marched into the doctor's office for postcoital testing, a lovely procedure that examines the mucus appearing a short time after a husband and wife—well—engage in coitus. Pre-testing, I abandoned romantic thoughts for pep talks directed at our sample: "Come on, sperm-mucus! Shape up and look your best for the doctors tomorrow!"

For the serum progesterone test, I submitted to a blood draw performed by the rookie lab tech who missed my vein but, rather than retreating for a fresh poke, fished around diligently under my skin until her tiny probe found its mark.

Finally, pre-medicated with Valium to sedate my cervix, I crawled up on the examining table for the tubal dye test, also known as the hysterosalpingogram, or HSG. In this gem of a test, a radiographic dye is injected into the uterine cavity through the vagina and cervix, creating a spill visible on ultrasound to confirm open fallopian tubes.

After having the HSG, I dressed quickly and made a beeline for the exit only to find myself—ears ringing and head spinning—back in the examining room with nurses issuing strict orders for me to lie down until the dizziness passed.

I had driven myself to the test and popped the Valium in the waiting room because I am nothing if not practical (why interrupt Mark's day to be my chauffeur?). Driving home while dizzy, however, had not factored into my plan.

Incidentally, the HSG test was the only one in which something weird—like nearly passing out—had occurred. My doctor chalked it up to nerves, but the episode formed a bit of a theory in the back of my mind, one I didn't dissect until later.

Experts say that the dye used in the HSG test boosts women's fertility levels for a few months, especially if the infertility is unexplained or caused by endometriosis. Mark and I seized this insider information and ran with it.

Other tests came later, along with fertility treatments, but we'd completed Step 1 in about six months. All testing, of course, was dependent upon my cycle, dependent upon the passage of time; another month, another ovulation cycle, another stretch of expectant trying, another phase of waiting, another menstrual cycle.

Mark and I toiled to the end of the "wait and see" path to behold the thorny road stretched out ahead of us. It was filled with white-coated professionals whose ministrations would muddle our marital bed.

And the testing had failed to give us a plan of attack. Sure, there was a touch of endometriosis on my part and a varicose vein on my husband's, but these were essentially non-issues according to our doctors: The varicose vein did not negatively affect Mark's sperm count, and my endometriosis was correctable with further treatment.

Experts slapped our infertility with the label: UNEXPLAINED. This diagnosis marked the end of wondering if my fear of remaining childless was silly paranoia. At the same time, our non-diagnosis rolled out the red carpet for doubt. Were God's plans for me—for us—truly good? Like walking out the door of a cozy house on a frigid winter day, reality smacked me in the face. My planning and striving had obstructed my ability to see God's ultimate power, and now I bristled at the stark truth: He was clearly in control, which meant that I was not.

The Trying

It's one thing for married couples to schedule time for intimacy, to set aside a space for connecting to ensure that making love doesn't get lost in our hectic lives. It's quite another to approach that appointment with secretarial efficiency and NASA-like precision, acting as if one's very life is balanced on adherence to mission protocol.

Our attempts at baby making required this sort of grueling accuracy. When the time was right according to my chart, the drill went something like this: Mark and I would have sex every other day for seven days. My apologies to Barry White, but a shelf abounding in sexy mixed tapes couldn't have transformed the focus of these meetings from performance to pleasure. This was a military operation.

After consulting both of our schedules, we determined a plan to meet in the boudoir on Monday, Wednesday, Friday, and Sunday at 21:00 hours to initiate delivery of male DNA material into female portal. To ensure optimal connection and proper transfer, the portal would then remain raised and stationary for 30 minutes, post-delivery.

This serious enterprise took place in an antique, four-poster bed within the quaint, sloping walls of our first home, a century-old fixer upper. Mark and I bought the house at a time when we were so full of hope it makes me tear up to think of it. We were in our late 20s and naïve to the lengthy trial that lay ahead.

Looking back, I want to sit down with that couple and tell them to hang on to hope and each other; I long to warn them about the lies that Satan will hurl at them in their first decade as husband and wife. Skillful deceptions like, "Your marriage was not meant to be," and, "You deserve this heartache." They need to hear the truth proclaimed with loud certainty: God's plan is to bless, so hold tight. This harsh season of despair will evolve into a show of God's faithfulness, as radiant and sure as the summer sun.

The Treatment

At the ages of 28 and 31, when Mark and I started pursuing medical treatment, we'd spent two years trying to conceive on our own. With a diagnosis of "unexplained infertility", we were optimistic about treatment. On the other hand, if no physical condition prevented us from getting pregnant, then why weren't we?

Having elected to follow the "natural family planning" approach after we got married, we were likely five years into infertility, rather than the two years that had passed since we started keeping track. Apparently, for TTC (Trying to Conceive) couples, natural family planning is 100% effective as a means of preventing pregnancy and 0% effective as a way to achieve it.

As I expected, we blew through six months of trying to conceive with the help of egg-making drugs featured in Step 2. I wanted to trust my doctors but intuited that transforming my body into an egg factory wouldn't solve our problem. If my ovaries were working properly all along, one egg a month should have done the trick years ago.

Step 2's supposed "mild" drug regimen was anything but. Anyone who spent quality time with me while I took the fertility pill Clomid could tell you I be straight trippin'.

In one week I churned out a semester's worth of inspired lessons and considered abandoning my baby quest to pursue the title of World's Greatest Teacher. The next week, I toyed with scrapping my hard-won master's degree to pursue motherhood come hell or high water. During the Clomid days, I trailed a wake of snappish remarks and angry outbursts. Grief seeped through my pores.

The whole world seemed to conspire against me, from the pregnant teen at the mall to the well-intentioned cousin who invited all moms and children to go first through the Christmas buffet line. And let's not forget the lab tech who performed an exploratory ultrasound without a word or a smile. Throughout Step 2, I was desperate for hope but too bitter to grab on to a lifeline anyone might have flung my way.

I can't entirely blame the drugs for coming unhinged, though. My loss of balance was also tied to my fierce desire to keep things normal. My mantra was "Fake it 'til you make it," and I continued to barrel through life while taking no prisoners. A model citizen at work, church, family gatherings, holiday parties, and baby showers, I showed up with a cheerful, if deranged, smile. And if a doctor's appointment/ultrasound/blood draw/procedure occurred in the middle of my workday—as it nearly always did—I left my gangly middle schoolers in the hands of another teacher, drove to the appointment, braved the procedure, and returned to my students with that same plastic grin.

For fear of missing timely information from my doctor, I answered phone calls at school, although most bore the same old news. Results of pregnancy test: Negative. If my students noticed my sporadic comings and goings, my frequent hallway breaks to compose myself, they had the grace to let it go. My closest co-workers—fellow teachers and American Sign Language interpreters—became my greatest cheerleaders and counselors, praying for positive test results and discreetly escorting me out of the classroom when tears threatened to breach the dam.

Our next treatment step, IUI (intrauterine insemination), was much the same but boasted an $800 price tag and, therefore, came with higher stakes. Insurance had covered the testing and meds up to Step 3, but with IUI we were on our own. Mark and I scraped together funds for three unsuccessful IUI attempts and then found ourselves at a crossroads.

The sticker price on Step 4, *in vitro* fertilization (IVF), was around $15,000. Five years into our marriage and even fewer into our careers, we had a mortgage, car loans, and student loans, and were slowly paying off credit card debt.

Was it responsible to consider shelling out this outrageous sum on a treatment with no guarantee? Mark and I could follow perfect protocol during the IVF process and end up with crushing debt and no baby. Did considering such an invasive treatment signal our lack of faith? After all, God didn't need assistance to make a baby. He placed one in Mary without the help of a husband, who's usually a key player. Surely he could produce a pregnancy in my defective womb with or without our involvement and without leveraging our financial security, our emotional stability, and the health of our marriage. Couldn't he? I prayed and pleaded and bargained with God. In despair, I challenged him to meet my emptiness with his power to fill me. And he answered me: Wait.

CHAPTER 2

Options and Obstacles

*I*f I had a nickel for every foolish word I endured while Mark and I were "trying" to have a baby, I'd spring for a small private island on which to exile all those fools. Jokes like, "Just take *my* kids for a night. That'll cure you!" and, "Are you sure you're *doing it* right?" Let's face it: Fertile Myrtles and Matthews don't grasp the humbling process of toiling away at God's directive to "be fruitful and multiply".

As an Infertile Myrtle, it's hard to buy the rosy statistics that say that of couples trying to conceive, 30% will get pregnant the first month, 59% within three menstrual cycles, 80% within six cycles, and 85% within a year.

Further projections state that a whopping 91–95% will achieve pregnancy within three to four years.[1] This is good news if you're trying to get pregnant! While the wait may be excruciating, the odds are in your favor. Our doctors assured Mark and me that this was true. Of course, friends, relatives, and even strangers were quick to offer helpful (and less-than-helpful) advice as well.

Here are a few of my favorite nuggets of non-wisdom:

1. "Your time will come!"

   One relative enthusiastically offered me this advice at the grocery store as she wheeled her second child, who was only days old

---

[1]   Kelmon, J. (2014, October). How long does it take to get pregnant? Retrieved January, 2016, from http://www.babycenter.com/how-long-does-it-take-to-get-pregnant

and still pink and downy, through the cereal aisle. I offered a weak smile, but my thought in the moment was, *Listen, Clueless, you don't know that!* Clearly, the prolonged experience of infertility did not make me Mary Sunshine.

2. "Oh, don't worry! It took us two/four/six/eight months to get pregnant. You should try herbal tea/massage/acupuncture/hypnosis/ standing on your head/Jamaica/sexual position A/B/C because it worked for us!"

   I just nodded my head during these monologues and tried to picture waterfalls and fields of daisies.

3. "Do your dogs sleep with you? Maybe you should get them out of your bed."

   It is beside the point that, yes, our dogs were sleeping in the human bed with us. Did these people suppose that Mark and I hadn't grasped how the baby-making transaction worked or that moving the dogs lying between us required too much of a Herculean effort? CAN'T...MOVE...FURRY...BODY...NOT...ENOUGH... STRENGTH. Apparently they did. Whether the canines shared our bed or not, our two Jack Russell terriers were decent substitutes for children until the real thing came along, and their tail-wagging and bed-snuggling provided more comfort than people's unsolicited advice.

4. "Relax!"

   This is my all-time favorite. It comes in a variety of flavors, including, "Have a few glasses of wine before you..." "Maybe you two should get away for a few days," and, "Just stop trying so hard!" Though nuanced, these jewels share the same underlying theme: "Step away from the crazy pills, barren woman. If you'd just stop freaking out, you'd be pregnant in a jiffy!"

The people offering us advice were not mean-spirited, they were merely oblivious to the miles Mark and I had already traveled in our efforts to achieve pregnancy. Quite against our will, we'd become experts in a field that we had no desire to explore. Having survived more than 24 failed cycles, we knew that sipping Chardonnay in Jamaica was not the answer.

One of my favorite apples of gold came from an uncle who got by on his sense of humor, since his body had given in to the indignities of multiple sclerosis years ago. He pulled me aside one summer day at a family gathering at the lake, where my cousins, knee-deep in the joys of motherhood, watched their children toddle about.

After asking me how "things" were going from his permanent perch on a mobility scooter, he said very seriously, "Sarah, maybe it would help to insert some playfulness into your lovemaking."

I smiled gamely.

"OK, Uncle Chuck, and how do you suggest we do that?"

"When your Aunt Judy and I make love," he continued, "we like to talk. She often says to me, 'Beige…I think we should paint the ceiling beige.'"

I chuckled at his attempt to lighten my mood and shift my perspective. Our situation wasn't as bad as it seemed. Unlike Uncle Chuck, I could still walk, and feed myself, and—well—make love to my husband. His point was right on target, but I gave it little attention in the midst of my pregnancy crusade.

The A Word

We couldn't navigate for long on the choppy waters of infertility without being confronted with "the A word." Yes, during treatment, I foolishly perceived the option of adoption as a last resort. Strange, since one of my best friends in school had been adopted at birth and her family seemed normal. In college, I had also walked with a teenage friend through her pregnancy and adoption plan.

Post-delivery, I watched Jodie hold her daughter in those first few hours and gaze at her with such love and longing I had to look away. Even though I was light years away from starting a family of my own, I sensed the ripping and tearing in Jodie's heart as she placed her newborn in another woman's arms. Grief clashing against joy.

This exposure to the dynamics of adoption took on much greater significance when infertility came knocking. Still, I considered adoption a desperate remedy. I wanted "my own" kids and concluded that shared genetics would give me more control over eventual outcome. Certainly, I thought, Mark's and my genes would guarantee us a child who looked, spoke, and acted like us. Our biological child would be reasonably intelligent and have an ideal mix of temperaments—between my introverted but people-pleasing tendencies and Mark's extroverted candor—and a proclivity for the electric bass.

Adoption was a beautiful choice for other people, of course. Just not for us.

If there was ever any inkling of doubt about my aversion to the A-word, an adoption representative with a serious public relations issue sealed the deal. You might say she was the crown jewel in a string of fools who sought not to understand but to generously share their own opinions.

While in the middle of taking a break from treatment, Mark and I attended a one-day infertility conference and drifted into an informational session on the topic of parenting through adoption. We were seated in the back row in the conference room when a graying, short-haired woman in a power suit stepped up to the podium. She appeared to be bringing anything *but* good news.

Shockingly, the rep did not kick off her presentation by announcing that the world's chocolate supply had vanished and happiness had been declared illegal (as I expected she would). However, she did dive in with condescension. Her diatribe went something like this: "If you are even considering adoption, you need to get used to the idea that your potential child will always have two sets of parents. You will never be the child's only parents, and you're just going to have to get over it."

Way to rub salt in the wound, Debbie Downer.

"Besides that, the adoption process is long and tedious, and you'll need to prepare yourself for a wait. It will be years before you bring home a baby."

Ten seconds into the session, I was ready to exchange my cushy seat in that conference room for a high top at the hotel bar. Who was this woman to attack a roomful of wounded couples, limping toward the shifting finish line of parenthood? There was a place for reality therapy, but this was not it. We needed words of hope and encouragement, not to be reprimanded like naughty children.

Along with the guilt that infertile couples heap upon ourselves (e.g., Should I be fasting/juicing/wearing looser pants/not trying so hard?), this chick seemed to imply that our barrenness was a mark of poor character and adoption the punishment for our sins.

This was the final nail in the adoption coffin for Mark and me. In our minds, parenting someone else's child was already a consolation prize, and the price of throwing ourselves at the mercy of venomous adoption case-workers was too high. With a monthly period reminding us of our failure and glowing pregnant women popping up everywhere, we needed support-ers, not critics. After enduring the rest of the session while fighting back tears, I swallowed the lump in my throat and did the only thing I could do. I snatched the workshop feedback form and scribbled a scathing review. I hope that woman got fired.

IVF

By the three-year mark, Mark and I had had our fill of waiting and trusting. We'd taken a break from treatment for a few months and hoped God would reward our restraint by granting us the baby we'd spent years asking for.

"Look how good we are, God!" I insisted. "We're trusting you to work all this out…so could you do it already?"

I'd like to say that this forced waiting made me into the picture of holiness, but I was as antsy for a baby as ever. We'd reached Step 4 in my plan—*in vitro* fertilization—and had taken out a home equity line to cover the cost. While our insurance would continue to pay for the drugs and ultrasounds required for *in vitro*, it did not cover the $5,000 egg retrieval and embryo transfer. Parting with that kind of cash was tough, but it was worse to sit idly by as my aging eggs lost more spunk with every passing birthday.

The *in vitro* fertilization procedure came in a variety of options, such as traditional IVF, GIFT (gamete intrafallopian transfer), or ZIFT (zygote intrafallopian transfer)? With GIFT, embryologists throw together egg and sperm in a dish but then place the mixture in the woman's fallopian tube (not into the uterus) to allow sperm and egg to pair up on their own. ZIFT is similar, but lab techs force the union of egg and sperm on the outside and then place the zygote—a baby in its earliest stages—into the fallopian tube. Unlike IVF, the potential success of both GIFT and ZIFT relies on healthy, unblocked tubes.

Louise Joy Brown, the first "test tube baby", was born thanks to traditional IVF in July 1978, and, since then, the procedure has been used to successfully bring more than five million babies into the world. Traditional IVF drops the mother's egg into the boudoir (a.k.a. petri dish) with the father's sperm, allowing the lovebirds to connect on their own, or embryologists force the connection by using ICSI (intracytoplasmic sperm injection), which is a fancy term for shooting a sperm directly into an egg like a dart into a balloon. Once the sperm and egg team up, the resulting zygote (baby embryo) is then deposited directly into the woman's uterus.

Since this was our first attempt, old-fashioned IVF was our treatment weapon of choice. Though not quite as effective as GIFT or ZIFT, it was a bit cheaper than those options and had a decent chance for success. Our physician, Dr. Dodds, was among the top five infertility specialists in the nation and his average success rate for an IVF cycle was nearly 50%. Since our current success rate was 0%, Mark and I were inclined to play his odds. We completed our consultation, shelled out our four-digit deposit and then prepared for takeoff.

The most difficult part of the procedure was the drug regimen (read: injections) and constant ultrasounds to determine how many follicles (egg containers) were ripening. This information would determine the appropriate time to give myself the mother of all injections, the golden-egg releaser. Sending my ovaries into hyper drive was a tricky process, which necessitated multiple trips to the doctor, daily blood draws, and self-administered, subcutaneous belly injections. I became so steeped in the lingo and operations of the Assistive Reproductive Technology (ART) world that I considered buying myself some scrubs and a sterile hair bonnet.

Still, I was convinced that this interruption of my day-to-day routine was no big deal. Most of the time, I envisioned the nurses in the delivery room, nine months down the road, laying our baby on my chest as Mark and I laughed off our brief stint in the world of ART .

HCG, the final egg-releasing hormone administered in an IVF cycle, is given via intramuscular injection. The 1 ½ inch needle used for the shot must be inserted at exactly the right time, preferably directly into the butt muscle. However, since I was acting as my own nurse and could, regrettably, not reach my own derriere, I administered the shot in the next best place, my upper thigh.

Usually, I turn my head when Nurse Ratched pokes me with a needle, but it's impossible to look away from the act of plunging a miniature jousting stick into your leg. Giving oneself shots is one of the many experiences unique to those of us trying to conceive. Thankfully, today's TTC generation can access YouTube's library for IVF guidance, where nearly 5,000 how-to videos remove all the guesswork from impaling yourself with a hypodermic needle.

My circa-1999 guidance for administering these shots was limited to a stapled packet of paper with 13 step-by-step instructions and charming clipart illustrations.

Step 1: Rub top of vial with alcohol pad to disinfect. *Duh.*

Step 2: Place needle on syringe. *A simple twist. Nothing to it!*

Step 3: Turn vial upside down and push needle through rubber stopper. *Got it.*

Step 4: Pull back on syringe plunger to draw up correct amount of medicine.

    Not to brag, but it frequently occurred to me that I should go to medical school because, well, I am objectively good at this stuff!

Step 5: Remove needle from vial and gently depress plunger until a few beads of medicine emerge from tip.

    I feel like one of those gutsy nurses on Gray's Anatomy

Step 6: Flick syringe to remove air bubbles. *Done! Wait, is that an air bubble? What happens if I don't remove all the air bubbles? Flick, flick, flick.*

Step 7: Remove and dispose of needle in sharps container. *Crap, I think I left that red plastic box in my car.*

Step 8: Replace with fresh needle. *Umm, another hand would be helpful here.*

Step 9: Rub site of injection with alcohol. *Again, another hand please?*

Step 10: Hold the syringe barrel tightly and use wrist to inject the needle through the skin and into the muscle at a 90-degree angle. *Angle? Do I need a protractor for this? Deep breaths.*

Step 11: Check the needle: Pull back on the plunger a little to make sure you did not hit a blood vessel. If blood comes into syringe, remove the needle immediately. Do not inject the medicine. You could die. Dispose of both the syringe and the medicine. Get more medicine in a new syringe. When you give the second injection, give it on the other side of the body.
  I mean...really? Medical school is looking less appealing.

Step 12: Inject medicine: Push down on the plunger. Do not force the medicine by pushing hard. Some medicines hurt. (*Are you serious, instruction guide? Thank you for that piece of enlightenment.*)
  Or, like me, you can shoot the liquid in with one swift movement to get this process over with.

Step 13: Once the medicine is injected, remove the needle at the same angle as it went in. Place gauze over the injection area. (*Whew. I feel dizzy. Where are the directions for treating hyperventilation?*)

My first actual attempt at this process left me puzzled. The needle bounced repeatedly off of my skin instead of gliding into it. After reading the directions again, from the top, I realized I had forgotten steps seven and eight, removing and replacing the original needle with a fresh model, sharp enough to pierce my skin instead of merely poking at it.

Finally, however, I did succeed. In 36 hours, that magical human chorionic gonadotropin elixir would prime my follicles for release and land me on Dr. Dodds's examining table for egg retrieval.

Egg retrieval was considerably more uncomfortable than that shot I fussed about a moment ago. Though my mind was in a drug-induced fog, I was awake during the painful procedure. Once home and back in my right mind, Mark regaled me with stories about my choice words and well-aimed kick that nearly took out a member of the retrieval crew.

About four hours after egg retrieval, an embryologist injected Mark's sperm—which were retrieved the same day through a much simpler process—into the eggs and checked the following morning for evidence of fertilization. The six embryos that resulted were cultured in the lab for three more days. Since our doctor did not perform selective reductions (the practice of reducing the number of fetuses in a multi-fetal pregnancy), he would only transfer into my uterus the number of embryos that I could safely carry to full term.

This is where the rubber meets the road for Christian infertility specialists and ART patients. Whereas many Christian ethicists and theologians reject the practice of IVF outright, they fail to consider the thoughtful ways in which Christian doctors are helping couples achieve pregnancy while maintaining the highest standards—God's standards—for honoring life. These were the conditions under which Mark and I sought treatment.

In addition, plenty of ethicists view assistive reproductive technology as antithetical to Christian beliefs about God's role in creation. Such perspectives sermonize that infertile couples should reject treatment to instead trust in God's timing and in his plans. But infertility, like arthritis, fibromyalgia, or cancer is a medical condition and Christians who seek discernment during treatment do not lack faith. In fact, relying on God to transform a pencil-point-size blastocyst into a baby can grow mustard seed faith into a giant redwood.

Dr. Dodds's staff readied our three pencil-point-size blastocysts for transfer and froze the remaining three for a potential future procedure. At least the transfer was a piece of cake, much like the turkey baster IUI procedure but with more precise placement in utero.

I returned home to lie flat on my back for the next two days and then soldier through the two-week wait before my pregnancy test. I dreamed of triplets.

The first two days I was on a mission: Lie still and encourage my embryos to take hold. I watched *Oprah*, read *Better Homes & Gardens*, and took naps. It felt like a scaled-down spa vacation. Forty-eight hours later, when I returned to walking, doing stairs, and being my klutzy self, I obsessed over the fragile little buggers inside me. A jostle here. *Are you OK, little guys?* A heavy step there. *Sorry about that! Stay right where you are!* Going to the bathroom was nerve-wracking. As I peed, I pleaded with my triplets. *Hold on tight, babies! I'll do this as quickly as I can!*

One moment I pictured my future, resplendent with three chubby pink faces, smelling of baby powder. In another flash, I anticipated the nurse's phone call briefing me with news of a negative pregnancy test. Expectation and despair jockeyed for position, addling me with emotional whiplash.

When the day of the test finally arrived, I scuttled into Dr. Dodds's office for the blood draw then returned to my middle schoolers. I was grateful to fix my mind on grammar and history and coping with general teen angst, which I could easily empathize with.

After school, I threw a ball for our two high-strung terriers and later fixed Mark's favorite, spaghetti and meatballs. If the news was bad, the pasta would at least comfort *him*.

As I strained the pasta, our kitchen phone finally rang and my heart dropped into my stomach. I gingerly picked up the receiver, my throat like dust.

"Hello?" I croaked.

"Is this Sarah?" a familiar voice asked.

"Yes, it is." I needed her to cut to the chase.

"This is the nurse calling from Dr. Dodds's office."

"Hi."

"I just wanted to call to let you know that your test was negative. I'm sorry."

"Oh. OK, thanks."

"Someone will be calling from the office in the next few days to discuss your options."

"OK, thanks."

"Bye."

Click.

Did she say "options"? It seemed I had just come to the end of those. I hung up the phone and slid down the wall onto the cool linoleum floor. At first a ball of annoyance knotted my insides, but that anger quickly unraveled into a powerful sadness that threatened to swallow me whole. After everything—the blood draws and ultrasounds, the shots and medications, the home equity line of credit, the following of every directive to the letter—we were right back where we started.

I felt like the stupid donkey who followed the carrot, trusting that its sweet crunch was just one step further. This failed IVF attempt had removed my blinders: our endurance did not guarantee us a baby. In fact, it seemed likely that continuing treatment would end in further loss of something I couldn't even name.

Through tears, I railed at God as I faced the facts. My body had reliably brought me from point A to point B for 30 years, but my womb was undeniably out of order. I sensed the canyon of emptiness inside me being hollowed out once again.

Then and there, I pledged to stop trying, but only a few days later, I phoned the nurse once again to schedule my next procedure. Surely the doctors could fix me.

CHAPTER 3

Marriage on Infertility

Barrenness sows seeds of insecurity in an otherwise healthy marriage like nothing else can. If left untended, these weeds can creep into the very bedrock of the relationship, much like vines crumbling the once rock-solid foundation of a house. Infertility compelled *me* to seek isolation, not relationship.

So where, pray tell, was my husband during all of this longing and loss? After all, marriages—even infertile ones—usually involve two people. Of course Mark wanted a family too. The youngest of six, my husband grew up in an Italian home where life revolved around *la famiglia*; How could he not want children? Having a family was one of the first things Mark and I discussed when it became clear that we were waltzing blissfully toward a fancy wedding and a forever marriage.

At the time of our engagement, we were both working toward teaching degrees and (obviously) adored kids. We planned to have three or four of our own after we finished college and had the chance to purchase a home and put down roots in a family-friendly neighborhood known for its excellent schools. Mark and I had always been good planners. And we were on the same page that Valentine's weekend years earlier when we decided it was time to start "trying".

Somewhere along the road of scheduled sex and failed pregnancy tests, though, Mark had lost his passion for the idea of having a baby. Yes, he went along for the tests and treatments and offered his physical presence and emotional strength during the hard times. But trudging through infertility side by side eventually became my dragging him along a path marked with my determination and his ambivalence. After a while, Mark saw what infertility treatment did to me. My mood swings and tendency to keep him at a distance made him eager to cut our losses and move on…while we still could.

Mark wanted me to have peace of mind; I wanted me to have a baby. Mark wanted financial stability; I was OK with accumulating mounds of debt for treatments that claimed no guarantees. I wanted a child no matter the cost. Mark wanted a healthy and happy wife, even if that was all he would ever have.

Infertility permeated our relationship and turned little issues into big ones. I remember my mom pulling me aside one fall day at their house to issue a warning.

"Don't be the Bickersons!" she exclaimed.

"What do you mean?" I asked, feigning ignorance.

She had noticed Mark and me airing our grievances with each other on a regular basis and with no consideration for the fact that we had an audience. I was horrified to think we had become "one of those couples," the ones that are better to avoid than to engage. In a moment of recognition, I wondered how many double dates our married friends had excluded us from because of our negative vibe. Mark and I had run far afield of the green pastures I'd envisioned for our first few years of marriage.

Meeting, dating, and marrying Mark had been an adventure. I'd met my match, and his attributes checked off every box on my "perfect husband" list. He was sensitive but strong and self-assured with a hint of rebel. Though we had different communication styles—his characterized by East Coast frankness and mine more Midwestern and mannerly—we clicked immediately. The Washington, DC area where I had moved to earn my master's degree was Mark's home turf and, after we met, he became my personal tour guide. My husband-to-be led me through museums and monuments as well as introducing me to the art of DC driving. When we were together, life crackled with spontaneity and excitement.

Mark was also romantic and musical, writing poetry and strumming along on the guitar as I sang. My Fender, a 21st birthday gift from my parents on which I was slowly learning chords, found a more natural home in his hands. In any case, if I had a boyfriend who played guitar while I sang, what need did I have to learn to play myself? I did, so I didn't. He couldn't carry a tune in a bucket, and my fingers were hopeless at plucking strings. Clearly, our most engaging music was to be made together. That was our jam.

And if laughter is the best medicine, I was at peak health during our courtship. Mark was not afraid to be goofy and found in me an enthusiastic and singular audience.

He also knew how to be chivalrous, opening doors for me and making sure that fresh flowers adorned the apartment where my roommate, Wendy, and I lived. I couldn't wait to stand in front of the church I grew up in—all decked out in white before friends, family, and our pastor—and say, "I do," to my man.

But far from those first expectant dreams, our marriage had taken on the sensibility of a business arrangement, with my scheduling all things baby making and Mark's dutifully showing up at the necessary times. I was hyper-focused on my treatment plan and progressing from one step to the next. Mark and I had started out with so much—a strong faith, mutual interests, a passion for music and the outdoors—and I had reduced our relationship to the functional, which, ironically, made it fairly dysfunctional, hence my mother's rebuke.

My husband stood faithfully by me for those years when I placed our marriage second in priority to having a baby and I never had the sense to doubt his unconditional support. In a very real sense, I had abandoned Mark. Yet even as I ignored his need for deeper companionship, he chose to stay.

For Mark and me, honoring our commitment to each other during infertility meant agreeing to disagree while we grappled with two distinct perspectives. In his view, having kids would be a bonus to the relationship we already shared, a perk that, given time, may or may not come along. And if it didn't? Sad, yes, but certainly not tragic. More tragic was the fact that his once outgoing wife had turned into a recluse who spent most of her time vegged out on the couch kept company by two terriers. The prospect of childlessness was not the end of the world to Mark. The thought of being married to a crazy dog lady was much scarier.

At the beginning of treatment, after I had spent three months on the go-to fertility med Clomid, Mark began to entertain—and even embrace—the idea of a life with just the two of us. As educators with nine-month school calendars, we could spend our summers teaching English in Spain or Columbia, or rent a villa in Italy and wow friends with our knowledge of vintage wines.

From my angle, the idea of a family of two was ludicrous. It was clear to me that Mark and I had a je ne sais quoi that demanded to be shared. We had hit the proverbial jackpot—two people from loving and stable homes, our parents still married to each other—and had so much to offer a child. How could we keep this familial bliss to ourselves? Doing so, I thought, would constitute hoarding. How dare we perch greedily upon our own little pile of treasure, refusing to share it with a wrecked world in need of stability?

I took time to picture that life—a life without children. Mark and I would grow older each year, marking time in our microcosm while our friends pursued the rewards of parenthood. The stages of their lives would be measured by preschool graduations and soccer games, science fairs and band concerts, marriages and grandchildren. For us, the weight of time's passage would be recorded in career accomplishments, gray hair, and the arrival of new aches and pains as the aging process marched on. Life as a twosome was a poor substitute for a life surrounded by our own tribe of sons and daughters who would grow up to create tribes of their own.

Mark's question was simple: "Why isn't what the two of us have together enough?" But this was the wrong question entirely. It was like the firstborn child asking, "Why do I need a new brother or sister? Am I not enough?" To me, the love Mark and I shared was not "enough" but abundantly more—more than could be expressed between just the two of us.

As much as I loved Mark, the prospect of a life without children shook me. What would happen if we turned our backs on the God-given desire to have kids and instead stuck with our family of two? Making this decision felt like leaping across a high chasm with no sight of the ledge on the other side. I was convinced that choosing wrongly—kids or no kids—would lead to the end of our charmed love story.

Sure, I claimed to trust God, to depend on him for our daily needs. But as months turned into years without a child, I took on the load of fixing our problem. This obsession pulled Mark and me further apart and drove a wedge marked "infertility" firmly between us.

I had lost sight of the purpose for our partnership, perfect in its completeness before God, even in the absence of children.

CHAPTER 4

A Zygote Is a Baby

Two months later, after my cystic ovaries had settled down from our first IVF venture, we were ready—or at least I was—to resume pregnancy efforts. For our second attempt at IVF, we decided on the ZIFT procedure, or zygote intrafallopian transfer. This fertility treatment put a two-day-old embryo—or zygote—directly into my fallopian tube. In theory (though this is not yet supported by research), ZIFT increases chances of pregnancy because it simulates natural fertilization by placing a zygote in the fallopian tube, where sperm and egg naturally come together, rather than in the uterus, the drop-off point for conventional IVF.

In what came as a surprise to nobody, the insurance provider that declined to cover traditional IVF also refused to cover our ZIFT treatment. Since both options carried a price tag of $12,000–$20,000, I was happy to opt for any edge that ZIFT might afford us as we racked up more debt on our home equity line of credit.

The second time around, we were at least familiar with the routine. The ZIFT protocol largely mirrored that of our first attempt, down to the fertility drugs, ultrasounds, blood test, and my beloved injections. This time, however, Mark decided to get in on the fun. As we stood in our tiny bathroom, I instructed him on how to administer that final injection, the fertility formula that would release my eggs within a few short hours. Because it was now Mark dispensing the shot, we were able to inject it into my upper hip (read: butt) instead of into my thigh.

As I focused on the artificial flowers twining up our bathroom wallpaper, I braced myself for the shooting pain that accompanied the intramuscular injection. My concentration was shattered, however, by the sound of Mark's baritone voice breaking through in the all-business tone of a vetted nurse.

"Just a little poke now."

I wheeled around before he could make his move, and we locked gazes for a split second before dissolving into peals of laughter. My teacher husband, equipped only with a five-minute lesson on administering infertility injections, had embraced the role of Florence Nightingale and repeated the only words of comfort he could immediately recall: "Just a little poke now."

Mark's words resonated with the tenderness of a caregiver, and his offering came at no small expense. My husband was not a fan of needles or blood. On occasion, he had grown lightheaded when forced to endure his own routine blood draws and injections. As we caught our breath through giggles, I noticed beads of sweat on his forehead. He was at least as nervous about impaling me with a needle as I was about receiving the poke.

I braced myself for the second go around. Within seconds, I felt a tentative jabbing at my backside.

"What's wrong?" I asked.

"The needle won't go in," Mark replied, staring at the offending weapon.

"What do you mean it won't go in?" I demanded. "You have to push harder. Don't worry about hurting me!"

"No, look!" he implored. "It won't go in!"

I watched as Mark struggled to push the needle in, but instead of yielding to the sharp point, my skin moved with it and then bounced back like stretched canvas on the white trampoline of my bottom.

Then I remembered. We had forgotten to replace the blunt needle with its sharper cousin after pulling the medicine into the syringe. As a veteran of injection administration, I had repeated my rookie mistake, and we found ourselves working with a dull instrument. Humbled, we grabbed a fresh needle, and Mark injected me like a champ.

When we hugged afterward, I held on for dear life.

Mark's nearness that night in our bathroom-turned-lab and his willingness to participate even when he was so torn by the process—of seeing me hurting and striving toward a goal I might never reach—was exactly what I needed. It told me that we were still in this boat together.

A couple days later, I revisited the painful process of egg retrieval. After that, doctors performed laparoscopic surgery to place three fresh zygotes into my fallopian tube. The recovery was longer with ZIFT—because of its surgical dimension—but knowing this made the two days of lying prone on my back more bearable since bed rest was necessary for recovery. I took the call from the nurse at home 14 days later, heart pounding, palms sweating, certain I was about to have a stroke.

"Congratulations, you're pregnant!" the nurse said.

I responded with an eloquent, "Uh, what?"

"You're pregnant," she repeated. "Your HCG levels look great! We want you to come back in for a blood draw in a couple of days to monitor HCG and make sure your levels are doubling, but you're definitely pregnant!"

I thanked the nurse and signed off, immobilized by this official news.

I'm pregnant! I'm pregnant? Wait…what do I do now?

Mark and I were three years into trying to conceive, and I knew how to handle the disappointment of negative pregnancy tests, but a positive test? Nope. I was unprepared for the mixed feelings, the shock.

Wasn't this good news? Why wasn't I jumping up and down? I learned later, when sharing my story with other women who'd been there, that the inability to rejoice with news of a pregnancy is typical for couples who've been jerked around by the dashed hopes of infertility.

After I hung up the cordless phone in our kitchen, I dropped my hands to tentatively cup my belly, the one that had betrayed me with each passing month.

There's a baby growing in there, I thought, immediately dismissing the idea as ridiculous.

I was determined to keep my hopes in check until I received a thumbs up on my next HCG test. Then Mark and I could uncork the sparkling grape juice.

A week later, the next test brought news that my HCG levels had more than doubled, and nurses alerted us to the likelihood that I was pregnant with multiples, probably twins.

Mark and I responded with tempered enthusiasm. Yes, this was our first pregnancy in three years, and so far, our problem had been getting pregnant, not staying pregnant. Still, we debated about whether to share the news or to keep it to ourselves. We sensibly agreed that the grown-up decision, of course, was to keep my pregnancy under wraps until we'd reached the first trimester milestone. Then we promptly started blabbing anyway.

We began to talk cautiously about a due date (February) and what color we would paint the nursery (buttery yellow). We tiptoed around the subject as if the budding life inside me was a broody teenager bent on running away. We used a lot of "if" statements, like, "If this all works out," and, "If we have twins." And at six weeks along, just when we were starting to drop the cautionary "if" language, a trickle of blood showed up.

We sped to the office for a HCG test and then waited at home for the call advising us that I was in the middle of a miscarriage. Only that's not what happened. HCG levels were normal and continuing to double, the nurse told us. Spotting is common for many women during pregnancy, she reminded us. We were to continue administering shots of progesterone in oil. All systems go.

We had dodged a bullet.

The next week, I was the maid of honor in my friend Marcy's wedding. After the spotting scare, news of my pregnancy had spread beyond our inner circle. My belly was not as flat as it had been when I was fitted for the maroon bridesmaid's dress three months earlier, and I thrilled at the thought of our growing baby. Even though I was only six weeks along, even though I was spotting, Dr. Dodds had given the all clear and I could practically smell the essence de infant that would fill our home come winter.

As I sat in the brick-walled banquet hall at Marcy and Pete's wedding reception chatting with the mom of an old friend, she asked me how things were going. I summed up the last two months and told her about the knot in my thigh, formed after daily progesterone-in-oil shots, which are required for sustaining an early IVF pregnancy. I had tensed up once when giving the injection, and oil subsequently pooled in my muscle, leaving a visible goose egg on my upper right thigh. The lump had been there for weeks, and no amount of heat or cold therapy got rid of it.

Nancy reached out sympathetically and placed her left hand on the knot like a butterfly alighting on a blossom. Our faces were within inches, Nancy's New Agey touch therapy intruding into my personal space. I attempted to fill the awkward silence with equally awkward blathering about the tedium of infertility, my ambivalence over this hard-won pregnancy. Once my initial discomfort eased, I realized Nancy was a masterful listener. She leaned forward into my story, undistracted by the music and dancing that swirled around us.

At the end of my monologue, Nancy lifted her hand from my leg as nonchalantly as she'd placed it there and said quietly, "I believe the lump is gone." And it was.

My analytical nature begs this question: How can a simple touch bring about immediate healing? Though I never asked, Nancy would likely credit the power of the Holy Spirit operating through her. For me, the experience stands as proof of a power we are unable to see but that is always working for our benefit. Nancy's healing touch was a glimpse of God's kind authority over our bodies that I would hold on to when my own pain blinded me to his goodness. And I would need this ballast sooner than I'd hoped.

One afternoon, a week later, I was scheduled for an early ultrasound, a routine test for women who achieve a pregnancy with procedures like IVF. At the ultrasound, my doctor would confirm that a baby was growing in my uterus and determine if I was carrying one baby or multiples. Mark and I would also hear the baby's heartbeat for the first time, the sound that signaled fast-approaching parenthood.

Once in the exam room with Mark, I donned the smart backless gown and assumed the position on the table with Mark by my side. We chitchatted with the doctor while he washed his hands and put on gloves and Mark and I waited for the moment of truth. I had grown used to this routine: my feet up in stirrups and butt exposed while conversing with doctors and nurses about the weather, weekend plans, and the latest news headlines.

The topics of conversation were so predictable with every doctor I'd encountered that I was certain all med schools dedicated a specific class to this art form: Conversational Topics during Pelvic Exams 101. I pictured socially awkward med students hyped up on coffee and pulling all-nighters to memorize checklists of acceptable subjects to discuss when the patient is flat on her back with her nether regions exposed.

Acceptable topic: We're going up north this weekend. Do you have any plans?

Unacceptable topic: Have you ever considered getting a bikini wax? 85% of women groom their pelvic region. Why not you?

Acceptable topic: How about this heat wave?

Unacceptable topic: I hear that Costco has a great new skin cream for eliminating stretch marks! Have you tried it?

Maybe the list of unacceptable topics was the more important one. Anyway...

My stomach did flip-flops as I pondered this list and waited to get a glimpse inside my uterus, which had so far shown less than stellar performance in the childbearing department. The doctor inserted the probe for the transvaginal ultrasound and shifted it about for reconnaissance. My eyes were glued to the screen searching the grainy shadows. I waited for the doctor to clue me in, but his face indicated only—confusion.

"Huh..." he said.

"Uh, what's going on?" I asked.

"Well," he continued, "I just want to make sure..." His voice trailed off.

I glanced at Mark, who looked as anxious as I felt. *Make sure?* A colony of butterflies had taken over my stomach.

"Make sure what?" I asked, trying to remain the proper patient but getting angrier with Dr. Young each second he left me in suspense.

"I'm sorry," he said. "I can't find a heartbeat."

Was he apologizing for his incompetence—for not being able to locate the heartbeat—or for something much worse?

"What does that mean?" I asked.

I fought to remain calm, not to lose my head, not to take the good doctor by the shoulders and shake him until he spoke sense. Surely rational words from a medical professional would fix this problem.

Dr. Young's shoulder sagged beneath his white coat and his head dipped to remove his glasses. Finally, he lifted his eyes to meet mine.

"It means," he said slowly, "that you have an ectopic pregnancy."

I heard the word "pregnancy" and latched on to it. The term did, after all, imply that I was still pregnant.

"An ectopic pregnancy?" I asked. "What's that?"

Dr. Young explained. With an ectopic pregnancy, the fetus develops outside the uterus, typically in the fallopian tube. In short, the pregnancy is not viable because, unlike the womb, tubes are ill suited for growing babies past about nine weeks' gestation.

I flashed back to the ZIFT procedure and to all the steps I had carefully followed since. Precise timing for oral medications and shots, follicle development and egg retrieval, the painstaking work of growing zygotes in the petri dish and the surgical placement of these zygotes in my tube. Why this seemingly simple glitch couldn't be fixed perplexed me.

So my zygotes got a little sidetracked, I conceded that much, but they were mere inches—about the length of a credit card—from their final destination. Why couldn't we help them along? Wouldn't a puff of air through a plastic stint or a gentle nudge from a surgical spoon do the trick? The doctors had a comprehensive protocol for creating a baby and placing it inside me, but they hadn't figured out how to troubleshoot zygote relocation just yet? Rage sliced through me. This small detail seemed like one God could've handled. Hadn't I prayed enough for this pregnancy? Hadn't I used the right words in my pleading?

After the ultrasound, Mark and I met briefly with Dr. Young to discuss what to expect from my body next and then bolted through the waiting room to the parking lot. My legs felt heavy as I lugged myself across the stretch of pavement between me and the car, with Mark hurrying ahead to get the door. Safely in the passenger seat of our Chevy Malibu, I buried my face in my hands and plucked tissues from the box on the seat between us. Mark put his arm around me, a hedge of protection.

After dropping me at home, Mark drove to the pharmacy to pick up the prescription for methotrexate. This medication—an antimetabolite conventionally used for cancer and arthritis treatment—would put a stop to my impossible pregnancy by keeping the embryos—our children—from growing any further.

"Are you sure you're OK for a few minutes?" Mark asked after escorting me into the living room.

No, I was definitely not OK.

"Yes," I told him.

"I'll see you in a few minutes." He kissed me tenderly on the forehead and, with a backward glance, rushed out the door to accomplish the task at hand.

I called my parents and sobbed into the phone, trying to explain this new development, an ectopic pregnancy, and also asking the central question: "Why?"

"Why is God doing this to me? Why did we come this far to have our dreams of a child snatched from us once again? Why did I let myself believe I would be a mom in a few months?" My parents offered as much comfort as they could from 30 miles away, but they struggled with the same questions, the same pain of God not meeting human expectations, not answering righteous prayers.

Suddenly, I felt sick and had to get away from the phone against my mouth and the too much talking in my ear. Before hanging up, Mom declared that she was on her way. I collapsed on the couch with our two terriers curled up against me. When Mark returned from the pharmacy, things had gone from bad to worse. My skin felt clammy and I was shaky and nauseous. I needed to get to the bathroom fast. As Mark helped me stand, waves of cramps gripped me and radiated from my chest to my pelvis. A high-pitched ringing filled my ears, and splotches of light and dark clouded my vision. I leaned on Mark to take the few steps to the toilet before I lost my lunch.

Once my stomach was emptied, I switched sides and sat down on the seat, clutching my belly. The coolness of the stool against my feverish skin brought momentary relief until I saw the blood. It was as if Dr. Young's diagnosis of a tubal pregnancy had given my body permission to drop its deception.

The intensity of the pain came as a surprise. Dr. Young hadn't prepared me for the cramping or the flu-like symptoms. Or maybe I had tuned out his instructions about what to expect while growing an embryo in a space the size of a coffee stirrer. The doctor's orders had seemed pretty straightforward that afternoon: Take the medication and the pregnancy would go away. We would glide right back to our merry lives of infertility. Yet here I sat, doubled over and sobbing as the throbbing spread up into my chest and down into my legs.

Surely the pain will pass, I thought. *I just need to lie down.*

Mark gently helped me back to the couch, where I collapsed and closed my eyes. There, I focused on willing this complication—my sudden and intense symptoms—away.

My mom arrived 20 minutes later and appraised the situation. Her daughter was in the fetal position, sobbing. Mom was expecting tears, of course—another bout of grief in a long line of negative pregnancy tests—but not the physical anguish. She and Mark helped me to the bathroom to throw up, and then I slumped down onto the toilet once again.

The ringing in my ears grew louder as my vision tunneled. The pressure in my abdomen felt like something was trying to push its way out. Even in my delirium, I recognized this was a ridiculous notion. The babies were in or near my fallopian tube and would not be exiting through the birth canal.

Mom and Mark exchanged glances and made a decision. We were heading to the hospital. I fought the urge to vomit as Mark sped down the highway with Mom following close behind. Once at the high-rise downtown, orderlies rushed us from the ER triage to an exam room where the smell of sterilized sheets and institutional plastic triggered me to wretch again into a kidney-bean-shaped bowl in my lap. By then, my tears had morphed into steady moans and pleas for someone to relieve my misery.

After the doctor on call quickly examined me and took my health history from Mark, my diagnosis was obvious: an ectopic pregnancy that wasn't going to disappear quietly with time and methotrexate. The nurse promptly hooked me up to a morphine drip, bringing instant relief. I made a mental note to send her a thank you note when I got home.

While I slept, the ER doctor called Dr. Young to schedule emergency surgery. When the halls became hushed and the lights grew dim, I realized that my dad had made it to the hospital. He and Mom, perched on either side of my bed, held my hands and prayed.

I later awoke to the sound of Mark and Dr. Young discussing the surgery, another laparoscopy. This time, the procedure would locate the "misplaced embryo/embryos" and remove them. For the surgical team, the task was simple. For me, letting go of my nearly two-month-old babies was impossible. Continuing to grow them would kill me, but knowing I would never hold them, I wasn't so sure this would be a bad thing.

Hearing this discussion, I issued a groggy request for the doctor to save my tube, if possible. I needed him to leave what was left of my reproductive system intact as a possible home for future babies. Even in a cloud of grief and physical distress, I was still preoccupied with doing whatever was required to have a baby.

The surgery was a success in that Dr. Young managed to save my tube by scraping the fetal tissue out instead of removing the tube. The whole intricate procedure was caught on film, so afterward I got to see the images of my bulging right fallopian tube, the place where, in fact, twin embryos had stopped to make their home. I stayed in the hospital for three days so that medical staff could monitor my HCG levels and make sure the numbers continued to fall. Since there have only been about 100 cases of unilateral twin ectopic pregnancies documented in medical literature, my case had become an intriguing topic of conversation around the hospital and a cause for scholarly discussion at the regular meetings held by the doctors on the fourth floor. http://ispub.com/IJGO/16/2/14212

As a result, I became quite a celebrity there, with nurses, doctors, and orderlies stopping by to see the woman who had carried twins in her tube and lived to tell about it. I tried to reward their visits with a winning smile and a shared chuckle over my bad luck in becoming a medical curiosity via this route. Deep down, I was disillusioned with my body's traitorous ways and sinking into depression. Why had God allowed me to become pregnant at all if my pregnancy was going to end with the death of two babies and a senseless map of scars all over my belly?

My parents continued to counsel me to pray, but praying made me feel even more impotent. I had no interest in being on my knees and at the mercy of an apathetic God.

"You can pray for me," I told them, "I can't pray for myself anymore."

God was gonna do what God was gonna do. If I stopped asking, perhaps I wouldn't feel so bitter about not receiving. If I refused to meet with God, perhaps he would fully grasp my desperation. Or maybe I felt ridiculous leaning on a deity who, in my eyes, hadn't shown up recently.

This was a poignant and gut-wrenching moment for my parents. They wondered if their daughter's faith had been discarded amid the rubble of lost babies and lost hope.

The day I was released from the hospital, I was physically and emotionally wasted. The sounds of construction work filled the streets of downtown Grand Rapids, and the smell of hot, fresh asphalt rose in waves. It was July, my favorite month in my favorite season. I longed to put my current heaviness behind me and to dive headlong into summer's carefree days. But once again, my best laid plans went astray.

CHAPTER 5

Leaving Behind

*W*e had a camping trip planned for just days after I was released from the hospital, and I was relieved to have something concrete to focus on. The weeklong trip to Pentwater required plenty of planning, including grocery shopping, packing, cooking, and checking the readiness of our gear. Were our flashlights equipped with fresh batteries? Did our camp chairs survive dry rot to serve another summer?

We had graduated from tenting last fall when we bought my grandparents' compact 15-foot camper, and we were thrilled (or at least I was) that we would be sleeping in a cushioned bed and cooking on a gas stove inside four non-canvas walls. The camper even had a tiny bathroom with a sink and bathtub.

Lake Michigan Camp at Pentwater was a special place. I had been attending the camp with Mom, Dad, and my brother, Craiger, since I was 12 and—once Mark and I had moved back to Michigan from Virginia— we made it a regular foray on our lengthy summer travel calendar. There's truth to the adage that the three best things about being a teacher are June, July, and August.

At Pentwater, we would be surrounded by friends and family at a time when we needed the relational support. We would also be away from home, where our house's vacant rooms had become a daily reminder of our own emptiness. In contrast, the towering pines, rolling dunes, and peaceful beaches of Pentwater had always been a manifest expression of God's vast power, as well as his love for me.

I could take a walk, sit in the dune grass at sunset, or sing around the campfire at night and know that God was real and not just some idea created by a bunch of men. Unfortunately, infertility made its presence known even here.

When I had left the hospital less than a week before reaching Pentwater, it was with doctor's orders to continue the methotrexate regimen, as well as to continue showing up at the lab for blood draws every other day to ensure my HCG levels remained in check. When I told Dr. Young of our camping plans, he simply asked, "Is there a hospital nearby?" When we promised to drive 20 minutes to the hospital in Ludington every two days, Dr. Young gave our annual trip his seal of approval. And so, somewhere between morning devotions and evening s'mores, we trekked into town to endure yet another test and then waited back at camp, with its sketchy cell phone service, for a nurse to give us the "all clear."

I spent much of the week curled up on the cozy couch in our 15-foot home-away-from-home. I napped and read as my initial plans for play and adventure dissolved into the reality of post-surgery exhaustion. Meanwhile, an undeniable realization accompanied my weariness: The dependable, soul-filling comfort I had come to expect from Pentwater had changed. The close friends I had lounged with on the beach and played volleyball with for decades were now engaged in other pursuits, namely parenthood. The last year had brought a torrent of babies, meaning that the couples with whom we normally played cards at the pavilion or shot the breeze with at the fire bowl were now busy feeding, cuddling, and playing with their infants. Mark and I couldn't dodge the reality that we'd been left behind.

I quietly calculated how far along my pregnancy would have been if my twins had settled in my womb. In mid-July, I would've been able to wave goodbye to the risky first trimester and start openly complaining about swollen ankles and shrinking bladder. Instead, I was nursing painful incisions and a constant cramping that was my new normal. Every twinge reminded me of my deeper hurt. I missed my babies.

When I felt well enough to come out of my shell, Mark would drag a camping chair out to the edge of our campsite, where I could observe

Pentwater's perennial circle of trailers. One day, my cousin Gina pulled her chair over to sit with me, her three-month-old daughter, Anna, on her hip, and asked if I wanted to hold her. Of course, this was a trick question.

Did I want to hold a baby? Yes, desperately. But I wanted to hold my own. The fact that I had failed so consistently and publicly to conceive over the past three years was both painful and humiliating. My pride prevented me from saying any of this to Gina, though. In the moment, I did the one thing I had mastered—putting on a happy face to make others comfortable.

I carefully placed my arms out in front of me, creating a cradle for Anna to signal my expertise in baby-holding. After all, since I couldn't get pregnant, my ability to handle an infant could also be called into question based on my lack of experience. Gina placed Anna in my arms, and I observed the long lashes, the puckered mouth, the distinct smell—a mixture of baby powder and breast milk—from an emotional distance equal to the span between Earth and Mars.

I loved Anna because Gina loved her, but I also resented the shift in our friendship that Anna's birth represented. I could empathize with the love that my cousin had for her daughter. It was, after all, precisely the kind of love that I was seeking. Yet, I noticed that, for my friends, crossing the bridge into motherhood precipitated a forgetfulness of the world before children and a lack of awareness that some people were still citizens of that world. I was on one planet, and Gina was on another, and our gravitational pulls were entirely different. Gina was drawn to Anna, and I was pulled toward self-preservation.

Over months and years of infertility, the dissonance between what young mothers had achieved and what eluded me created, in my mind, an explicit distance between us; whether consciously or not, I had succeeded in building an austere wall around my affections. In a bit of irony, few women even noticed the pre-emptive blockade to our friendship—because their relational needs were met with or without me. Still fewer strapped on ropes and climbing gear in efforts to scale that wall in pursuit of earnest connection.

The Sunday after we returned from Pentwater, I was sitting on one of our long, orange pews when Pastor Stacy asked everyone to stand while she recited the closing prayer. Mark was in the front of the sanctuary with the worship team while I stayed seated, willing Stacy to wrap up the service quickly as I fought another wave of nausea. With the final "Amen," I sprang out of my seat and experienced a familiar ringing in my ears. I staggered through the side doors as bright spots danced in my eyes and I fell to my knees in the grass. My friend Linda arrived just in time to see me throw up in our church's side yard.

"Are you OK?" she asked. "I just sent Becca to get Mark."

Becca, her daughter, was part of our church youth group, which I led. Neither of them knew about the tubal pregnancy. None of our church friends did. As active as Mark and I were in our small church—leading worship and youth group and revitalization initiatives—we had managed to keep this secret.

Church was one place where we could demonstrate our competence, one place where infertility didn't rule. We didn't want to burden the struggling congregation and our beloved pastor, who had enough worries. Worries like replacing the old roof and the worn orange carpeting in the sanctuary as well as compelling more people in the door each Sunday were enough to wear everyone thin. But it was time to come clean.

"Tubal pregnancy," I muttered as Mark arrived to the mess and knelt on the ground beside me.

"Let's get you home!" Linda stated decisively. A middle school teacher, Linda was difficult to rattle.

She was all business now and prepared to take me on as her charge. She eased me into her car, and she and Becca drove me the few blocks to our house while Mark packed up his guitar. Linda deposited me on the couch on our back porch, and I thanked them tearfully. When Mark rushed in the door, Linda and Becca graciously excused themselves with a promise to bring dinner the next day.

My body seemed to hit the replay button, revisiting the day more than two weeks ago when we discovered my tubal pregnancy. The nausea, light-headedness, and abdominal pressure returned and Mark and I headed back to the emergency room to tackle the problem. I wanted it over with. The frequent visits to the hospital, the shuffling around like a senior citizen waiting for my incisions to heal, the chatting with the clinic med staff more than I gabbed with my best friend. It was all more than enough. And since there was no baby that would result from this pain, I wanted whatever was left of my tube removed so I could return to pursuing life as a healthy 30-year-old woman. It was hard to believe my own actions—my own drive to have a babe in arms—had created this summer of chaos. I fumed in silence as we barreled down the highway.

We didn't have to wait long this time since we were kind of big stuff at this hospital ("Hey look! It's the lady with twins in her tube!"). Cue the morphine as my pain had once again become intolerable. A quick blood test revealed that my HCG levels were on the rise when they should have been declining, a sure sign that fetal tissue (no longer actual babies) continued to multiply in my right tube, causing it to bleed out.

Again I went to the mat with God on this significant detail. OK, so he wouldn't bless my attempt at a pregnancy. No baby for me. The message was received loud and clear. But could he perchance minimize some of the suffering along the way? I knew, of course, that he could intervene and reduce this multiplying tissue to nil without all the fanfare, so why didn't he? Even after I had promised to cut off communication with God, these pleas still wended their way to the Almighty.

Apparently my right tube was a champ at incubation. The brutal paradox was not lost on me: I had spent the last three years trying to achieve pregnancy, and now I couldn't seem to get un-pregnant. Another surgery was in order to get rid of the threat—to my long-term physical health as well as my sanity—once and for all. This time, there was no question that I would have to surrender my entire tube.

I endured another laparoscopic surgery and received VIP treatment from the entire staff, who by now saw me as a sort of poster child for disastrous tales of infertility. I stayed in the hospital for another week, submitting to HCG tests multiple times a day. By day seven, my levels had finally fallen and stabilized, and Dr. Young gave me the thumbs up to head back to the couch on our porch. A posse of supporters and admirers flanked me as the nurse pushed my wheelchair out the revolving front door, where my faithful husband waited.

My 30th birthday loomed a few days away, and my mom, the inveterate party lady, was determined to make it a cause for celebration. In her eyes, there was no problem so large that food, festivities, and a gathering of rowdy merrymakers couldn't solve—or at least obscure for a while.

She felt powerless to fix my longing for a baby and had made up her mind to provide a birthdaypalooza that would kick my grief to the curb for a few hours. Once I gave her the go-ahead to plan the party (with one stipulation: no children), Mom made last-minute phone calls to friends and family. My parents readied Songbird Ridge—their quaint home and 10-acre spread—for the event.

When Mark and I arrived on that sunny July evening, the pool shimmered, the deck welcomed guests with its soft chairs and umbrellas, and a smorgasbord of cocktail shrimp, canapés, and fresh fruit beckoned. My parents met us with quick hugs when we pulled up their steep, wooded driveway.

"We borrowed Nancy's karaoke machine for later!" Mom whispered excitedly. She had pulled out all the stops.

In view of the summer that wasn't, and despite a few girlfriends who spent the party poring over their baby books, the celebration was just what I needed. Friends showed up from far and wide to rally around me and say in so many words, "We've got your back." My colorful friend Tami, the life of every party she'd ever attended, who taught with me and became my vocal coach for a short time, was there. She was joined by Renée, my best friend since middle school. We had been on the cheerleading team and weathered bad perms and even worse boyfriends together. Also at the celebration were a smattering of aunts, uncles, and cousins who supported me simply because we were family, and perhaps because my mom was notorious for her shindigs.

As the evening wore on and the partygoers headed home, the handful of stragglers broke out the karaoke machine and sang our hearts out under the moonlight. I threw my head back and forth, relishing the curtain of hair that swirled wildly around me. The deck became my stage as I lifted my voice loud and long and raucous to the trees and my pulsing mosh pit of friends.

The jangling chords of '80s glam rock filled me and drowned out the ache, resurrecting the younger Sarah, the woman unbowed by infertility. The moment was a flash—a carefree island plopped into an ocean of loss—

but it beckoned me closer to the truth. Was it in my power to seek more angst-free moments like it? Sure, the treatment and waiting had taken a toll on my mental health and my relationships, but I was still young. I could decide how the next few years played themselves out, Lord willing, and I was not inclined to allow my future to be stolen away by an endless barrage of medical procedures or a looping cycle of grief.

As I grasped the mic and rocked out to Mötley Crüe's "Wild Side" while friends boogied and swayed around me, I felt my load lighten as a scintillating idea came to light: I had a choice about what to do next. Now was the time to see what else was out there in the world and to live a life free of the manic hope and abject discouragement that came with trying to conceive. It was time to take a break from treatment and my baby fixation to see what other bright possibilities lay ahead.

Although Mark had passively supported my treatment decisions so far, he was visibly relieved when I shared my new plan: A stretch of time with no talk of infertility or treatment to make room for the return of sanity and peace. I didn't know if this chapter would last six months, a year, or more, but we would spend the time being young and happy and letting nature take its course. Who knew? After everything Mark and I had been through, we could end up pregnant on our own. Stranger things had definitely happened.

I couldn't take a break from fertility treatment, however, without pausing to say goodbye to my babies, my tenacious twins who had dug in and caused so much trouble. No one else could see this truth, but they had made me a mama. I knew God held them in his arms, probably squirming and making a fuss, in anticipation of my arrival. Even though my babies had left earlier than I expected, God had certainly knit them together during those eight weeks of pregnancy and that alone gave their lives meaning, even if God's purpose would never be mine to understand.

I imagined my twins—a boy and a girl—who would have been best friends and archenemies as well as they grew up and sibling rivalry set in. When Craiger and his wife, Lori, learned of the loss of our twins, they gave us a garden stone. It was etched with an angel who carried two infants in her arms. I placed the gray slab on an easel on top of the china cabinet in our living room, a reminder of our babies' short but treasured lives, and gave them the names that had come to me unbidden: Grace and Gabriel. Grace. God's unmerited favor—a kindness that we can do nothing to earn but only receive as a gift. Gabriel. An angel messenger.

It was only in hindsight that I recognized these names as reminders of God's kindness, God's boundless desire to communicate his love for me.

In my darkness, God continued his pursuit. *I am good. I am with you. Wait.*

CHAPTER 6

Free Rangers

*A*s I mentioned before, while Mark could've made the leap to living permanently childfree with relative ease, he never even considered that option for a second. But deciding to put off infertility treatment was as freeing for both of us as it must be for free range chickens that escape their cages to roam about pecking at grubs and stretching their little chicken legs.

For the past three years, our cage had consisted of doctor's appointments, procedures, and a frustrating attachment to my menstrual cycle. As free rangers, we could shed these tedious confines and spread our wings to embrace life as a couple. Romantic date nights, weekend road trips, and even spontaneous sex held tantalizing potential.

The trick involved scrapping our "childless" couple label—the one that smacked of deprivation—and trying on a new "childfree" persona. We could simply be a man and wife embracing each day as a family of two with the ability to pursue their own agendas. These agendas might include living in a tiny house with a composting toilet, teaching English in Italy, or purchasing a goat farm to produce our own feta cheese. There is an entire movement out there that is positively passionate about, well, the *freedom* that comes with a childfree lifestyle.

Childfree couples proudly brandish this badge of solidarity. They balk at the term "childless". "Why?" you might ask, and they will reel off their reasoning. "Childless" implies that one is missing out on something and the "childfree" crew definitely is not. In fact, their lives are filled to overflowing with more personal freedom, money, time, and energy than their parenting counterparts. Who wouldn't jump at the chance for these perks?

In fact, every August, the creators of International Childfree Day recognize amazing kid-free people and their accomplishments in an effort to spread awareness. Yes, the childfree lifestyle is on the rise and—for many—it is not a cause for sadness but celebration and an invitation to a broader conversation.

A broader conversation? Mark and I could certainly relate to that. Our friends had become experts at using anecdotes about their children as substitutes for stimulating adult conversation. It amazed me how they could force such stories to apply in every situation under the sun. Take the following discussion topics, plucked from snippets I've heard over the years, as cases in point.

Careers: You should see our little Cody with his blocks. We are just sure he's going to be an engineer someday!

Religion: Kylee's baptism is coming up. Should I *buy* a baptism gown or have my grandmother fashion one from my silk wedding dress?

Literature: Oh, I don't have *time* for reading, but Owen loves *Brown Bear, Brown Bear*! We have to read it at least twice before he'll go to bed!

There's no participating in conversations like these; it's more a matter of becoming an innocent bystander as the art of mature conversation devolves into debates over Huggies versus Pampers.

From where Mark and I stood, there was no question that many of our friends had fashioned their children into little household gods, idols whom they'd built their lives around. Although it's likely we would have unknowingly joined them had we become parents so easily, for now my inability to participate in parenthood alongside them kept me at an envious distance.

The idea of trying on an alternative lifestyle, one that made the world—and not parenthood—my oyster, was both fascinating and appealing. I decided to treat this time as an anthropological study, going undercover to become a member of the "childfree pack". Yes, I was obviously childless and adopting the swagger that came with being childfree would require some training. First, I would need to carefully study my subject.

Initially, I imagined a childfree life involved owning a 4,000-square-foot home with plush white carpet, jetting off regularly to Fiji or Bali or Belize, and indulging in daily cocktail hours during which Mark and I could finish our drink orders with the words "shaken, not stirred." As it turned out, however, there was more to the lifestyle than I had envisioned.

According to my research, free rangers pledged allegiance to the childfree movement for several reasons. First, children are expensive. Paying for diapers, formula, Little League, and Ivy League all add up and take away from other pursuits, such as buying bottled wine (instead of boxed) or jetting off to the French Riviera.

Secondly, childfree couples cite the problems of overpopulation, pollution, and resource scarcity. Every year, 18 billion dirty diapers end up in landfills, not to mention plastic string cheese wrappers, juice box straws, sandwich bags, and the lasting treasures found in McDonald's Happy Meals.

Further, Many childfree couples simply rebel against societal norms for having children (the "you-can't-tell-me-what-to-do" approach). Some even think of procreation as narcissistic, a selfish quest to create a tribe of "mini-me's".

Perhaps the most compelling reason childfree couples put forth for not having kids deals with the unfairness of bringing children into a world filled with suffering. One must admit the idea of sparing a child from cancer or a terrorist attack is easy to buy into.

But who knew that the most basic of all human endeavors—procreation—was such a hot-button issue?

For the record, I believe this over-emphasis on the cons of having kids is a bit too much navel-gazing. It leaves out a discussion on the potential good each human brings to the world as well as each individual's inherent value in the eyes of God. If couple A is lucky enough to have a choice about their fertility and opts to remain sans kids, there is nothing morally wrong with this decision.

Likewise, if couple B populates their home with enough kids to host their own reality TV show, more power to them. Since God is ultimately in charge of the final outcome of our best laid plans, perhaps more seeking of his will and less of our own would do everyone some good. If I had learned anything from my years of running full force into walls it was that God would not prevent me from exercising my own will. But he *would* offer guidance when I invited him to lead the way.

We can find many of God's signposts in the Bible, and when it comes to having children, the story of Adam and Eve in Genesis can point those debating its morality in the right direction. In a few short verses, God encourages Earth's first couple to be fruitful and increase in number, as these gifts are blessings from him. As far as I know, God did not include an addendum, stating, "…and by the way, beware of overpopulation or parenting blunders that could create the next Jack the Ripper."

To be sure, God has entrusted us as responsible stewards of every good gift, including children, and equips us to care for them. And it is God who busily works out the more colossal problems of the universe—namely sin, which he has already had the final word on through Jesus Christ.

Childless or childfree? In my view, our attitudes play a huge role in shaping our perspectives and making the mighty mental shift from being a victim of infertility to seeing God's kindness in its benefits. This simple, four-letter change can illuminate possibilities that self-pity or grief may have obscured. In this way, the childfree perspective was a lifeline.

Reframing my infertility was my objective for the months following the summer we lost the twins. Stop waiting for a baby to arrive to participate in my one and only earthly life. Shop. Road trip. Soak in the bath. Explore new restaurants with our foodie friends (kid-less friends and those who still maintained grown-up lives after kids), date Mark, dive into juicy novels, power walk, create music. Quit pining for a baby. Just live.

From this one decision, my life went from gray to blooming with color. I came to realize that the parts of me I had long neglected during IVF treatment were still there for the taking. My love of travel and teaching merged as I became the architect of a trip to New York City, where 60 students visited Times Square and the Statue of Liberty and sat in orchestra seats on Broadway to watch an American Sign Language (ASL)-interpreted performance of *The Lion King*.

After experiencing the goose bumps of a Broadway performance, I began working with Grand Rapids' Circle Theatre to bring ASL-interpreted theater experiences to Northview's 50 deaf students and over 100 of my hearing students who were learning ASL as their second language. I dived into this effort and was rewarded when I watched my deaf students lean forward in their theater seats, mouths open and eyes wide, drinking in stories on stage told in their native language.

In March, I landed a role playing the deaf protagonist, Sarah, in Circle Theatre's summer production of *Children of a Lesser God*. Mark and I had never made any concrete decision about how long our break from treatments would last, but with my role in the play, the decision was made for us. We had a couple months before rehearsals began, but making an IVF attempt in the last few months of school would have been nearly impossible, not to mention ill-advised. Even if we achieved an IVF pregnancy, what if there were complications and I needed to go on bed rest? What if I experienced another tubal pregnancy (I was at high risk even without my right fallopian tube) and ended up darting in and out of the hospital all summer?

Now we had to look at the bigger picture. Community members would be filing into Circle Theatre in August and September to see the play. The opportunity to play the lead in a show so uniquely in my wheelhouse was rare and there was no way I could allow infertility drama to sideline me.

I crawled into the role of Sarah like it was a second skin and opened up to a band of compatriots in the Grand Rapids Theatre community. We spent every evening rehearsing and then headed to the Cottage, a local pub, where Mark joined us for late-night noshing and conversation.

Most of my new pals were single or married without kids, so our discussions centered on grown-up topics, like which restaurants served the best tapas in town and who in the acting community was a shoo-in for the next leading role. Not once did anyone pop the question Mark and I had been asked 100 times in recent memory: "So, when are you going to have kids?" Our rap sessions were sometimes trivial and sometimes profound but always illuminated the truth that our life did not have to be defined by our inability to have children.

Reed, the actor who played Sarah's husband, James, was a high school music teacher who conducted multiple choir concerts and directed two musicals every year. Rachel had a day job, but her passion was Japanese dance, which she performed regularly with a troupe from the Urban Institute for Contemporary Arts. Marcus, who was deaf, taught sign language and dabbled in the ancient Irish customs of his grandmother. It was a brand-new world this community of adults, who, at least for now, had opted for pursuits other than raising children, and from what I could see, these quests were every bit as fulfilling as parenthood.

The play opened on a Tuesday night to a full house and, in spite of my anxieties about being such a rookie, received dazzling reviews. Opening night was monumental for those loyal to the theater community as any show's success or failure rested squarely on a smooth first run. The show's kick-off was always followed by a champagne reception. After changing into street clothes, I nervously made my way to the reception on the patio, where I was stunned to find a crowd bubbling over with excitement and appreciation.

Joe and Rodney, the guys who had encouraged me to audition for the role, met me with hugs and roses and asked what had taken me so long to become a part of the theater scene. Others greeted me with champagne and congratulatory pats on the back, and I basked in the glow of their praise. Over the two-week run, family and friends came from everywhere, brought flowers, and called me a star—someone they were proud to know. At these times, infertility existed only as a word, a puny little bug I could ignore or squash on the sidewalk beneath the shoes of my reclaimed life.

I have to admit, I could see why people found the childfree lifestyle so appealing. I could easily envision the years ahead with only myself and Mark to answer to, setting lofty goals every year, like running marathons in every state of the union or sailing around the world. These were adventures that would be too expensive and too time-consuming with children.

Perhaps this life was a bit narcissistic. Then again, what about the time and resources that would open up for other more selfless pursuits, like serving in youth and music ministries or taking mission trips? The summer's events had caused me to hit the pause button on my accustomed way of thinking.

In an award ceremony not long after closing night, I accepted a Grand Award for my role in the play. Though I have little recollection of it, I made my way through the darkened house to the stage, climbed the steps in high heels, and delivered my acceptance speech. The after party was full of congratulations and well wishes and my overwhelming sense of gratitude. As

Mark and I danced and carried on with friends we had made over the summer, there was not a thought in my head about what I was missing. My life was full, and I now recognized the opportunity cost involved in dwelling on losses.

We arrived home in the wee hours of the morning after hopping from one pub to another with the cast and crew of *Children of a Lesser God*. The play had snagged a bevy of awards, including Oustanding Play and Best Director. In contrast to the summer spent bobbing in and out of the ER a year earlier, my 31st summer had been exquisite and my immersion in the play was the pièce de résistance.

That September marked 16 months since my tubal pregnancy and, in that time, Mark and I hadn't "tried" to conceive apart from enjoying each other sans an ovulation schedule or treatment protocol. Among other things, we had spent the past year house shopping. While we hadn't outgrown our first home (purchased four years earlier), we had invested our blood, sweat, and tears in the 100-year-old farmhouse, and it was time to flip it. My first memory of our little two-bedroom, one-bath Cape Cod was of pulling up the living room carpet an hour after signing our mortgage to find classic, if a little neglected, hardwood floors.

My parents were there to snap a picture of us kneeling on the dust-covered boards holding a bottle of champagne between us, our smiles stretched ear to ear. Many discoveries followed that one, including four layers of wallpaper in the kitchen, an old brick chimney encased in drywall on the upstairs landing, and a small colony of bats that had taken up residence in the attic. One weekend, after Mark had blocked the bats' only entrance and exit, we came home to find them swooping from room to room like a scene from Hitchcock's *The Birds*. Mark joked that with the constant fixing and renovating, he often felt like we lived in a fort like the ones he'd built in the woods behind his house when he was a boy. In our short time in the starter home, we had demolished walls, painted and re-floored nearly every room and added a gas fireplace.

Along with the sweet memories of so many firsts, our entire infertility struggle had taken place within those four walls, and we were ready to move on. We wanted a larger house in a quieter part of town with a little less upkeep and a little more elbow room. We ended up with a five-bedroom, three-bath ranch in a wooded neighborhood filled with kids. Our new home was almost three times the size of our first, and it seemed to be an unspoken agreement that neither one of us had abandoned the idea of adding kiddos to our family of two. Our year off had given us new perspective, and we felt strong and prepared to take on any challenge.

We had three frozen embryos from our IVF attempt in 2000. This trio of babies was just chilling on ice, and it was time to thaw them out and see if they would take. Before we'd even hung pictures or emptied boxes in our new home, we called Dr. Dodds and scheduled our next IVF transfer for November.

Being free rangers had been an adventure, but Mark and I were unlike many in the childfree bunch who viewed children as excess baggage on the ride of life. If the trip could be so packed with thrills with only the two of us, how much fuller would the journey be with another along for the ride?

CHAPTER 7

The Decision

When Mark and I signed on for our frozen IVF cycle, our case nurse informed us that many women find FETs less stressful because the worry about producing stellar eggs and grade-A embryos is off the table: embryos are ready and waiting. Plus, the idea of a frozen embryo—though scientifically cool—brings to mind bags of peas and corn in your grocer's freezer. How would you like your embryos, fresh or frozen? You can't help but giggle. Even without these images dancing across my brain, I still had a semi-casual attitude about our frozen transfer in light of the years we'd spent enduring more tedious infertility treatments. I'd survived two rounds of comprehensive IVF and a tubal pregnancy; this frozen transfer was going to be a cakewalk.

The procedure represented our last paid attempt at making a baby. Mark and I had run out of cash, as well as the gumption, to put ourselves through more treatment. The golden summer of living childfree had given us a glimpse of the Promised Land. It was a life without the word "trying" in the context of starting a family. We knew that life could be abundant even without a baby and could yield more than an empty bank account and constant grief.

As a child of the '80s, I was compelled to draw on Yoda's sage words, which held extra import in our situation. "Do or do not; there is no try." We were ready for the "do." I didn't know it then, but a subtle shift had taken place; my drive to make a biological baby with Mark had been ousted by my desire to simply become a parent.

Besides being disenchanted with infertility treatment, I'd formed a theory about our 628.9, which is the medical code for "infertility, female, of unspecified origin," or "unexplained infertility." My own investigative work (read: surfing the web), coupled with personal experience, led me to hypothesize about the root of my infertility.

Twenty years earlier, when I was 12, I had nearly died during an undiagnosed and traumatic bout of appendicitis. When Mark and I eventually recognized that we were unable to conceive, doctors made a hysterosalpingogram (HSG) one of our very first infertility tests. As I mentioned, the HSG is an X-ray test that peers into the uterus and fallopian tubes and the surrounding larger abdominal cavity. Specifically, the radiologist looks for dye to spill freely out of the tubes to indicate that these baby pipelines are, in fact, open. As in most plumbing schemas, healthy tubes should allow for unrestricted flow.

My HSG had been uneventful and yielded normal results (dye streaming through tubes and into abdomen) except for the fact that I nearly passed out in the waiting room after the procedure. About 15 minutes later, my symptoms had dissipated, and I headed home thinking, *Huh! That was strange! Maybe I'll zip through the drive-thru for a milkshake!*

The second piece of evidence supporting my appendicitis hypothesis involved information we gleaned from the multiple laparoscopies I'd received over the past four years. In each of these surgeries, a miniature camera set out on an exploration of my abdomen. Though doctors failed to identify any connection between our infertility and the architecture of my internal organs, every medical report on these fiber-optic safaris included comments about the abundance of scar tissue found inside my abdominal wall.

I'm no med student, but statements like, "Omental adhesion to bladder, dense," and, "The omentum was adhered to the anterior abdominal wall and to the fundus of the uterus," didn't strikes me as positive. In my infertility scrapbook, I had a notable "backstage" photo that Dr. Dodds shared with me after one of several exploratory laparoscopies. It showed my greater omentum, a large apron-like fold of peritoneum that hangs down from the stomach, and it appeared my "apron" had been traumatized. Thanks to the rupture of my appendix and the spread of bacterial poison throughout my body, there was a two-inch hole all the way through it.

In my mind, our ectopic pregnancy delivered the final piece of evidence for pinning infertility on my appendicitis. Why had two healthy embryos stopped in my fallopian tube instead of traveling the short distance to my uterus, which is their natural path? Our doctor posited that fertility meds sometimes reverse the natural flow of the embryo's travel from tube to uterus. Sure, Dr. Dodds was technically the expert, but I had a different inclination.

Inside the fallopian tubes are tiny hair-like structures called cilia. In normal fallopian tubes, cilia have the essential job of pushing the embryo along through the tube to its final destination in the uterus. I had found stories online of fallopian tubes, cut open and examined after surgery, in which the cilia were frozen in place instead of being loose and flexible. The cause of this? Infection—exactly the condition that afflicted my insides during that 24-hour period when a burst appendix nearly killed me.

Picture a thriving coral reef in all its colorful vibrancy, with orange fish darting freely in and out of the swaying sea anemone. Now picture a haunted forest whose trees are black and unmoving, trapping any innocent forest creature trying to make its way through. This was how I imagined the difference between happy, healthy fallopian highways and my own post-apocalyptic tubes.

While concluding that my tubes were worthless might seem depressing, I found comfort in having a concrete idea of what might be causing our infertility. Unexplained infertility leaves the door open for all kinds of self-blame and loathing (e.g., "It's my fault," or, "I never should have…"). On the other hand, identifying a physical source of our struggle, in the form of defective fallopian tubes, allowed me to leave all of that pointless recrimination in the dust. No one was to blame for my wayward appendix, and I couldn't undo the damage that had been done. I could, however, use my newfound understanding of my tubes' shortcomings to determine the value of specific infertility treatment.

Our frozen transfer was one way of doing this. The procedure would bypass the one pesky tube I had left and plop the embryos right where they needed to be to grow into healthy, full-term babies.

The frozen transfer was completed mid-November and went off without a hitch. The only thing unfamiliar about it was the scenery. I had become used to passing the days after IVF in our tiny bedroom with the flowered wallpaper and the sloping ceilings. This time, I was in a new bed in our new bedroom in our new house, which we'd moved into just two months earlier. Aside from the novelty of my surroundings, the routine was pretty well trod. Stay in bed for two days except to use the bathroom. At least the bathroom was only steps away this time, instead of down a flight of stairs. It sounds luxurious, doesn't it, being ordered to stay in bed for 48 hours when you're not even sick?

But the grass is always greener on the other side of the hill. I'd been here too many times, and even the soft warmth of a down comforter grew old. There are not enough magazines, books, or Netflix in the world to make lying on your back for two days at the mercy of your potential progeny seem appealing. My butt fell asleep, and my lower back ached. Normally no fan of running, my legs begged for an opportunity to sprint around the block. I rested fitfully, and my frequent naps were plagued by strange dreams that woke me up to a cold sweat.

One afternoon, I awoke, burrowed under layers of covers like a chipmunk in winter, overheated and shaky. *Ridiculous,* I thought. I was perfectly healthy yet had probably boiled my recently defrosted babies from the inside out with my obsession for staying warm in a 67-degree house. I immediately called my nurse-friend, Wendy, to ask her if overheating my embryos was even a possibility. After consulting with Anderson, her doctor-husband, they both calmly reassured me that my fears were unfounded and certainly not documented in any medical journal. In hindsight, Wendy demonstrated sincere friendship by listening to gibberish about microwaving my children *in utero* without implying that my sanity was slipping away.

The Results

It was the moment of truth. Eleven days post-transfer, I was home from teaching by 3:15 p.m. to wait for the phone call with our test results. So far, I'd kept anxiety at bay by channeling it into frenzied activity—dishes, laundry, cleaning, checking e-mail—but my to-do list was done, and all that was left was the waiting. It was still not my forte.

This cycle had not been overly taxing, and over the past few weeks, I believed I'd kept my expectations in check.

As I waited for the call, though, it became clear that I hadn't been able to fool myself. I was fully invested in this last-ditch effort and would be crushed if it didn't result in pregnancy and, more importantly, a baby. August would be my due date, and I'd decided to take off the first few months of school for maternity leave. For me, this expectation before expecting always accompanied treatment. A little bit of optimism is like a runaway train.

The phone rang, and my heartbeat accelerated. I murmured a cautious hello into the receiver and braced for news from the other side. The nurse repeated words I'd heard time and again from my parents, my friends, and my church family.

"I'm sorry."

The frozen embryo transfer now qualified as another loss. The nurse droned on, but I caught only snippets: "Don't know why," and, "Sometimes this happens," and, "Discuss further treatment." I don't remember saying goodbye, but I hope I managed to be polite. Our infertility was not the nurse's fault, and, for perhaps the first time, I even released myself from responsibility.

I ran into the room that Mark and I were beginning to furnish as a nursery and my knees buckled. I wept at the walls and the white crib—what had possessed us to buy a crib, anyway?—and at the closet that hung with a miniature layette from well-meaning friends. Mostly I wailed at God. Tears rushed down my cheeks and spattered onto my jeans. I cried, slack-jawed and head pounding, until saliva pooled beneath my tongue and flowed down my chin and I lost my breath and became faint. I beat my fists against the ground and levied insults and accusations at my God, who was supposed to be in control of every single thing. Assuming God was all powerful, I couldn't fathom why he wouldn't just get over himself and throw a little blessing my way. Yes, I had finally absolved myself of responsibility for our inability to conceive, but I was miles from forgiving God for the injuries Mark and I had sustained at his hand.

This is what crazy looks like, I thought, *a tantruming child in a grown-up's body.* I had come unhinged.

My tears finally tapered off, and I waited for the sputtering to cease, too, so I could fill my lungs again. I was overwhelmed with exhaustion and something else. It was a feeling I couldn't quite put my finger on. Perhaps the white flag of surrender raised for a God I had not yet fully trusted but was about to. Instead of the sting of defeat, I felt strangely relieved. *I am not in control.* A rush of calm followed this thought, like the cozy drowsiness experienced seconds before opening one's eyes after a full night's sleep.

I stood up and loosely observed my body moving, walking out of the room and toward the kitchen. My hands reached to open the top drawer—the one with the pens and pencils and takeout menus—and pulled out the thick phone book. I opened the book and flipped instantly to the first section of the Yellow Pages, in the A's. My pointer finger took on a life of its own, jabbing the page and sliding down to its mark: Adoption. The largest ad on the page might as well have been a Las Vegas billboard with a flashing arrow pointing towards my new goal.

I carried the open book to our bedroom, where I picked up the phone from its cradle and punched in the number from the ad.

I paused to take note of my folly. It was 4:50 p.m. on a Friday in mid-November, and I expected a human being to pick up the phone? Even for a Christian organization, as this agency presented itself, this expectation was a bit lofty. As I listened to the rings on the other end, I pictured all of the office workers cutting out early to do some Christmas shopping or buy groceries for their Thanksgiving feasts. This 11th-hour initiative was pathetic. I knew that I should hang up and try again on Monday.

But wait. A pleasant, lilting voice answered on the other end.

"Adoption Associates, this is Carol. How can I help you?"

It wasn't even a machine but a real live person. After recovering from the initial shock that someone had answered the phone so close to quitting time, I quickly explained our situation, my business-like tone belying the puffiness of my eyes.

As I spoke to Carol, I noted that I'd left Crazytown behind and become calm, cool, and collected in a matter of minutes. This newfound repose had something to do with this phone call and a decision I'd made, though I wasn't sure how or when. In hindsight, I can see the transformation. The painful shaping that took years but appeared in an instant, like lightning slicing through the night sky. God had removed my heart of stone and given me a heart of flesh. His desires had become my own.

Carol talked to me like an old friend who bore good news. At the time, I was short on such friends. I wanted to invite her shopping.

I could hear Carol's smile when she explained what Mark and I could expect from the agency.

"You called at an excellent time!" she said. "We actually have more birth mothers working with the agency than we have families who are waiting to adopt!"

My jaw dropped to the floor. More birth mothers than waiting families? This sounded like a headline from *National Enquirer*. Everything I'd heard about adoption pointed to an agonizingly long wait for an infant, especially one born right here in the U.S.

Carol's perky Michigan accent continued, "This is a really good time to adopt. We have an informational session next Tuesday. Would you like me to sign you up?"

Next Tuesday? That was just four days away! I gave Carol a quick yes, and she promised to pop a packet of materials in the mail so they would reach us by Monday.

I sat on our bed for several minutes contemplating this turn of events. I was done trying to trick my body into giving me what it couldn't. Fed up with shots and ultrasounds and writing checks for treatment that would've paid higher dividends if we'd used them as kindling for our woodstove. Every single procedure had been a gamble in which the house won, and I was tapped out.

I mulled over the phone call and this tug that pulled in a new direction. I was skeptical that closing the door on one dream and opening a window on another within the same hour would be easy, but there it was. I was reminded of Jesus' words in Matthew, inviting the weary and burdened to come to him. "For my yoke is easy, and my burden is light," he had said. I felt a buoyancy I hadn't since childhood.

I didn't have to wait until Monday to receive the packet from Adoption Associates. It arrived in a manila envelope the very next morning, thick and authoritative and full of promise. I sat at the kitchen counter with a cup of tea devouring every word. I'd talked to Carol on a Friday afternoon and the package had made it from Adoption Associates' office 30 miles away to my mailbox the very next morning. It was a sign we were heading the right way. That the U.S. Post Office got the package to me through one-day delivery, and at no extra charge, might even constitute a miracle. I didn't know it then, but this minor feat was the precursor to a series of events that could only be ascribed to God's pre-eminence.

For nearly five years, my will had battered itself against the wall of God's sovereignty. The process was not pretty, but it was holy work. Before infertility, I had only paid lip service to this God I professed to follow. He was a convenient little deity whom I had relegated to the backseat of my life. For 32 years, I'd called the shots and expected his benign approval for my self-reliance. Infertility had shattered these lies and illuminated the ironclad truth of my impotence and God's ultimate power. I'd been forced, finally, to scrap my carefully devised plans for having a baby and take the plunge into a deeper faith that I could no longer fake.

This wild new trust felt like leaping from a plane without a parachute. I had become a speck and God was the vast blue sky opening all around me. Stepping to the edge, I closed my eyes. And fell.

CHAPTER 8

Plan A

𝓘 can't tell you how many times adoption came into my mind only for me to eject it promptly. I *can* tell you that this happened often enough to indicate that my newfound enthusiasm for the idea evidenced divine intervention. I had had plenty of valid reasons to dismiss adoption as an option for Mark and me, not the least of which was the pervasive attitude of society that adoption remained inferior to having a family "the old-fashioned way."

Along with that unfortunate adoption workshop two years earlier—the one in which the speaker mauled the hopes and dreams of every couple in the conference room by highlighting the agonies of the process—the general ignorance of pretty much the entire American population both intimidated and worked against us.

After all, Luke reminds us that out of the abundance of the heart the mouth speaks, and demeaning jokes about adoption abound. There's the story about the kid who does something to embarrass his parents. Without missing a beat, they lightly respond with, "Oh, he's adopted." Of course, there's also the sardonic misconception that counsels infertile couples to adopt in order to guarantee conception—"Just adopt. Then you'll get pregnant!"—which treats adoption as some sort of FDA-approved infertility treatment, an impersonal means to an end.

Fortunately, I did have a few wise friends and family members who recognized adoption as a worthy end in itself and encouraged us to pursue adoption because it was the right choice, not the last one. My mom had brought up the topic years earlier.

"Have you and Mark talked about adoption?" she asked. "You just need a baby. Who cares whether it comes from your belly or someone else's!"

This progressive mindset was typical for my parents, who had an abundance of friends who weren't related to us by blood but might as well have been. Mom and Dad had spent their days in small town Otsego, Michigan, doing life with colleagues, church family, and even their mailman. The fact that these people could not be called cousins, aunts, or uncles didn't diminish the intimacy that my family enjoyed with them. This clan showed up for each other at weddings and funerals, parades and fish fries. Isn't this what family did?

My therapist—who I like to call my "life coach" because I gained practical problem-solving strategies from her, not just couch time—also urged me to view adoption in a new light. I'll never forget the session when Jan challenged me with this question:

"Are you and Mark related by blood?" she asked.

Obviously not, I thought. Was I paying $80 an hour to someone that ignorant? Mark was my husband, and I was fairly certain Michigan outlawed marriage to a blood relative. Then I grasped Jan's point. Mark—my soul mate, the one to whom I had happily pledged my life, the most important human relationship in my adult life—was not, in fact, related to me apart from a piece of paper called a marriage license. Mark and I had joined our lives together forever through a choice, not an arbitrary tie to the same bloodline, and we had the freedom to bring a child into our family in a similar way. I could've slapped my forehead and shouted, "Eureka!"

Had I consulted God's take on adoption years earlier, I wouldn't have been so shocked. The New Testament lays out God's plan to adopt his people not as a last resort but by design and from the very beginning. In fact, Ephesians 5-6 states that the Lord "predestined us for adoption to sonship through Jesus Christ, in accordance with his pleasure and will—and to the praise of his glorious grace, which he has freely given us in the One he loves."

Almighty God had the power to make us his children solely through the rebirth we experience through our active acceptance of Christ's death for us on a cross. After all, he had given us his only son, an extravagant gift beyond human comprehension. But God didn't stop with our redemption. He chose not only to save us but to *accept us as his own* through adoption. God's infinite compassion and grace is the difference between rescuing a drowning man and taking that rescued man home to join the family.

Our creator desires a relationship with us, not of creditor and debtor but of father and child. Such is God's heart for adoption.

Though I am in awe of the transcendence of my father's vision now, my understanding of adoption when we started out was limited to what it would bring me: a baby.

As for Mark's heart for our new plan to adopt, I was the executive secretary of the operation and he followed along dutifully. Like many husbands, for Mark the prospect of change did not produce shouts of joy.

When he arrived home after our last failed IVF and my first contact with Carol at Adoption Associates, he pulled me into his arms and asked, "So, how are you feeling?"

"I'm actually OK," I said, pulling away. "Guess what!"

Mark looked at me quizzically. "Uh, what?"

"Well… I called an adoption agency today and talked to Carol and she said they have more birth moms than waiting families and she's sending us a packet and there's a meeting in a few days." I gulped in a breath. "I signed us up, OK?"

I looked up at him hopefully, aiming for puppy dog eyes. Mark dragged his hand through his hair and raised his eyebrows.

"When is the meeting?" he asked.

"Tuesday," I replied.

"OK, I'll put it on my calendar."

Mark may have been slow to get excited about jumping through more hoops for the adoption process, but his enthusiasm later would more than make up for his half-hearted start. Besides, his stoicism over seven years of marriage had provided an indispensable counterbalance to my frequent volatility. When I chased after silly whims—like scrapping my master's degree in education to become a realtor—Mark wisely pulled me back to reality. When he became too practical—foregoing steak dinners to pad our savings account—I pushed him to dream a little. We obviously needed each other.

And it didn't take long for Mark to see that the adoption process was not the same as infertility treatment, where our efforts amounted to nil. From that first phone call to Carol, each step sped to the next, like an elaborate set of dominoes we only had to tap to set in motion. Infertility treatment had brought a progression of closed doors. Our decision to adopt seemed to fling doors wide before we'd even knocked.

That is not to say that completing the adoption process was simple.

After the initial info session came the five-page application—which we completed at almost superhuman speed—and then the consultation, a private meeting with a supervisory staff member who reviewed principal adoption issues and acquainted us with the agency's policies and procedures.

Next was the home study, which strikes fear into the hearts of many potential adoptive parents. This screening and educational process claims to prepare and qualify families for adoption but feels more like a police interrogation in a dark room with Mommy and Daddy-to-be in the hot seat, squinting at the bright overhead light. Successfully completing this probe into our personal lives should have qualified us to raise a busload of children, not just the one baby we were hoping for. Mark and I were both educators with degrees and certifications to prove our childrearing potential, but the home study made us feel like imposters a' la Milli Vanilli.

To be fair, our home study worker, Michelle, was kind and approachable and counseled Mark and me to be ourselves. "We visit your home simply to make sure it's safe and that you have room for a baby," Michelle reassured us. All the same, the weeks before our home visit, I washed windows, scoured floors, and organized closets with Martha Stewart-like enthusiasm. When I was finished, our house sparkled like a photo spread in *Better Homes & Gardens*. It would likely never be this clean again if a baby took up residence, I mused.

In February, we met with our caseworker, who interviewed us and completed a report, included with the home study, which discussed our motivation and understanding of adoption, social history, marriage and family lifestyle, and child-rearing philosophy. Honestly, it was all a little much. In the past four years, I had stood in line at Walmart behind pregnant teenagers and witnessed screaming women in parking lots dragging their dirty children behind them like an afterthought. Who was making sure *these* people were child-worthy?

See, I still had a few questions for God and was guilty of daily spiritual amnesia. The road to parenthood had been rough. But in addition to the obvious treasures of family and friends, I had experienced millions of blessings in my lifetime—the chorus of cicadas and peepers that lulled me to sleep, the smells of moist earth and hyacinth marking the end of a long Michigan winter, the trails of light that painted the night sky every August during the Perseid meteor shower. These glimpses of my creator were only a handful of the multitude I hadn't taken time to count. What's more, I had done nothing to deserve these gifts. Why, then, did I continue to tie the blessing of pregnancy to my own righteousness instead of to God's generosity?

The lens through which I viewed others—and thus myself—was faulty, but it had started with a distorted perspective of God's immense grace. The Almighty's capacity to bless other women with pregnancy did not cancel out his power to consecrate my life. To see others with the grace God intended, I had to release myself from blame for our infertility and cleave to the life God had waiting for us.

The last step in preparing for this new life where we would become adoptive parents was the "profile." A nifty three-page piece of marketing, it told an abridged version of the Rollandini life story and would help to match Mark and me with prospective birth parents. The profile was a fun exercise that helped us to clarify our thoughts about each other and our reasons for adopting. We purposefully selected pictures showcasing our youthful vigor (since we anticipated that any birth parents looking at our profile would be at least ten years younger than we were) as well as our skilled ways with children, which were second only to Mary Poppins and Bert.

The first page of our profile showed Mark and me standing in the snow in front of our ranch-style home, each holding a dog. The second picture was of me snuggling with our two-year-old niece, Maddy, as we shared a book. In another photo, Mark strummed the Fender in front of the woodstove in our basement. In the crown jewel, our extended family perched by a split rail fence, surrounded by fallen leaves and just-picked pumpkins, the epitome of a warm, welcoming Midwestern family.

Armed with paper cutters and tape runners, we spent a wintry Sunday afternoon around Mom and Dad's oval dining table assembling our 50 profiles. Even my 80-something grandparents got into the act, feverishly trimming and sticking photos and creasing the folds to perfection.

In addition to our profile, ready and waiting for any birth mother who walked through the doors of Adoption Associates, we created our own piece of marketing. Adoption Associates included a $7,000 fee waiver if we BYOBM'ed (Bring Your Own Birth Mom) instead of the agency connecting us with one. So we welcomed the agency's oversight in creating a neon green half-page flyer advertising our desire to be parents. The flyer featured the bold headline "Option Adoption" and a photo of a chubby-cheeked baby. On the bottom was a 1-800 number and a pin number that would allow a birth mother to connect directly with us.

We posted the flyers in libraries, gas stations, Laundromats, and grocery-store community boards, hoping our baby's birth mother might notice it and reach out to us. Honestly, this approach to landing ourselves a baby-mama felt a little smarmy and a lot contrived, but adoption experts reassured us that the method was totally legit, and Mark and I had made a pact to leave no stone unturned. Somewhere between that initial phone call to Carol and the creation of our profile, Mark had jumped into the role of expectant father.

The first indication of his excitement came one night after our weekly Taco Tuesday. I was washing the dishes and cleaning up the kitchen—a chore we usually tackled together—when I realized Mark was absent.

"Mark?" I tried quietly.

Then again a bit louder. "Mark?"

"In here!" he bellowed.

I followed the sound of his voice into the nursery where Mark knelt on the floor with a tape measure.

"What's up?" I asked.

Mark paused from his measuring and looked up. "I was thinking," he said, "that we should rip up this old carpet and put in some wood laminate."

"Oh kay…" I replied hesitantly. This new and fully engaged Mark was a welcome surprise.

Mistaking my bewilderment for doubt about the worthiness of his proposal, Mark rushed on.

"Laminate would be much easier to clean—spit up and dirty diapers, you know—and it would be healthier for the baby."

I nodded my head dumbly as a lump formed in my throat. I swallowed hard.

"Yes," I agreed. "Let's do it."

Mark smiled and for a moment I was taken back to our younger years when his cocky grin and easy laugh stirred a fire in my belly. I took his face between my hands and planted a kiss on my lover. Before we ripped up the carpet, there might be just one more piece of business to attend to.

Waiting Parents

We completed our adoption orientation in November and were officially waiting for a birth-parent match by April. In those five months, we could've completed a couple of IVF attempts, which would likely have left us right where we'd been four years earlier. With the adoption process, Mark and I knew we were closer to having our baby than we'd ever been—that even with the inevitable twists and turns, we would finally be holding a child in our arms.

In April, the only thing left to do was wait. Our caseworker informed us that being matched with a birth mom would probably take nine months to a year, although many couples waited longer.

This time around, there was no pill to take or procedure to purchase to hurry the process of becoming parents. We had no (legal) options for getting to the head of the adoption waiting lists. I'd done my part and—in my mind—it was time for God to do his. I realize the hubris of this statement now, but at the time it made perfect sense. God had called me to relinquish control and I'd plunged into this newfound freedom with abandon. I was giddy with expectation. It reminded me of my middle school self, sitting in a comfy chair, turning page after page of a Trixie Belden mystery. With our decision to adopt, God had the immense responsibility of bringing all of the pieces of the story together to a satisfying climax and conclusion. My only task was to keep reading.

CHAPTER 9

It's All Good

"Everything happens for a reason!" countless well-meaning folks shared in their attempt to console my husband and me during our years of infertility. After losing our twins, I stared blankly at friends who tossed such flippant precepts my way. Their "It's all good" attitudes intensified my pain and provoked in me a sense of injustice.

Perhaps worse were my fellow believers who quoted scripture reminding me to trust in God's will. As a Christian, I knew this comforting drill all too well. These sound bites tasted sweet but smacked of judgment on the receiving end, inflicting more pain in the form of self-recrimination. I wanted to flee from these false representations of Christianity, from the idea that all would be well if I just kept my chin up. If there was purpose in suffering, why did so many endeavor to paint over others' pain in bright primary colors?

At the same time, four years of barrenness and losing our twins had hurled me into a depth of suffering I found meaningless interpreted through the world's increasingly humanistic lens. I had sought every rational solution to our problem and come up empty-handed. In fact, empty.

God had denied me the shiny pink lines that snake their way up third-trimester bellies, but his close presence with me throughout the journey had spurred a similar burst of growth, not physical but spiritual. He had freed me from the illusion that life was under my control and ignited a deep compassion for other hurting people, a compassion that I lacked before my own experience of loss. He had also opened me to the idea of loving a child with whom I did not share DNA. These outward signs of God's inner workings were undeniably good.

But as we launched ourselves into the adoption process, full of faith, I wondered what form God's goodness would take next. Should I brace myself for further suffering—the possibility of not being selected by a birth mother or being sucker-punched by a failed adoption—or would God's kindness reveal itself in a baby, bringing the closure and healing I yearned for? Though I sought to trust God's next move entirely, I prayed fervently for an end to grief. I was ready to be the girl who opened the presents at the baby shower.

On a sweltering day in late July, Mark and I got the phone call from Adoption Associates—the "You've been chosen" call. We'd been expecting a wait of at least six to 12 months, and waiting only three for this call was a cakewalk compared to the lengthy season we spent camped out in infertility purgatory. I was bubbling with excitement and sick with anxiety at the news. Although my confidence in God's providence had grown, I hadn't quite been able to kick the worry habit.

That evening, Mark and I met my parents at Aries café in Plainwell to celebrate. As we sat at the table in the front window etched with the restaurant's name, Mom and Dad presented us with a congratulatory gift: a colorful plastic Elmo guitar with lights and sounds and buttons for the baby to push—the perfect trinket for the parents whose goal is to raise an over-stimulated child right out of the gate.

The four of us shared a celebratory glass of Riesling, but it kind of bugged me that my parents were acting like this baby was as good as ours. Mark and I knew better that optimism could be dashed in an instant. My brain continued to shout, *Wait, wait! Don't get too excited. You've been close to becoming a mother before and look what happened. Don't make a fool of yourself by acting as if this adoption is locked up!*

Eight years into marriage, I was still wedded to the notion that tempering my deepest desires with constant doubt might prevent catastrophic disappointment, or at least aid in a more speedy recovery from injury. Infertility had made it nearly impossible for me to put on any semblance of rose-colored glasses. It's not that I didn't believe God *could* bring us a baby;

it's just that so many times he had chosen not to. And the whole command "Don't worry about anything"? I hadn't figured out how to follow those directions in real life. By age 32, I had become cynical in a way that I never thought possible. Sarah the cheerleader, the optimist, the "positive attitude changes everything" girl had not been able to remedy our childlessness.

Still, the tiny truth that we'd been "matched" with a birth mother roosted in the back of my mind. It beckoned me to believe that Mark and I might soon take on the "frazzled parents" roles our friends had assumed years earlier. The idea that someone had viewed our profile and identified us as desirable parent material at least called my cynicism into question. A woman somewhere out there had seen our picture—our story—and thought, *I can't parent this baby, but this couple could.* This small step forward, a connection with a birth mom, did not land us in no man's land, which is where we'd spent the last few years. No, knowing that a birth mom called the agency to set up a meeting with Mark and Sarah Rollandini was definitely a signal. It represented a small, hopeful possibility that I had to assimilate into my years of practiced wariness.

According to the agency's initial report, our birth mother was, in fact, a birth couple, seeking parents for their child. Their names were Nita and Tim[2] and they were 29 and 31, respectively, only a few years younger than Mark and me. Nita had a 10-year-old daughter, Jenna, from a previous relationship. The fact that Nita and Tim were not teenagers but full-fledged adults in a committed relationship left me scratching my head. Why would this couple choose another couple—not so different from themselves—to parent their baby? Considering the energy and cash Mark and I had sunk into our family planning efforts, the idea seemed absurd. Did God know what he was doing here or was this some kind of trick?

Even with my thoughts racing, when Mark and I arrived home from dinner, I shuffled through the house, opened the nursery door, and took a few steps in. The only piece of furniture—a white crib in the corner—didn't look nearly as threatening as it had six months ago. My heart quickened as I surveyed my four-walled canvas, and a smile escaped. The bird, dog and

---

[2] Out of respect for individuals who have invited Mark and me to be part of their adoption journeys, the names of birth parents have been changed throughout this book.

duck wallpaper border would have to go, along with the joyless tan walls. Our first meeting with Nita and Tim was two weeks away. Would they like us? More importantly, would they choose us?

The answers to these questions tarried, but we could not. Welcoming a baby into our home would require more than dreaming; it would require action anointed with elbow grease, which just so happened to be my forte.

"I'm ready," I whispered. The baby was due in October and—after nearly five years of waiting—we had less than three months to prepare.

The Meeting

On a humid day the second week of August, we motored 30 minutes south of Dorr to Applebee's in Kalamazoo for our first meeting with Nita and Tim. I was thankful that our caseworker, Shelley, would be there for the initial visit to grease the skids. Mark and I were, after all, meeting in a casual restaurant with strangers to discuss a topic that was anything but casual. Nita and Tim had a baby on the way, and we desperately wanted to be parents. No biggie.

On the way to Applebee's, the agency called with news that Shelley, our caseworker, had pulled over on the side of the highway to toss her cookies onto the concrete median. Since our caseworker was out of commission, the agency secretary asked if we wanted to reschedule. Nope.

As daunting as the task before us seemed, we couldn't stomach the prospect of waiting a few more weeks to learn if this couple was our match made in heaven. My sweaty palms rendered me barely able to grasp the phone to my ear. Nonetheless, I calmly informed the secretary that we were going to fly solo and launched a few arrow prayers, missiles of jittery phrases strung together.

Fifteen minutes later, we marched into the restaurant and, seeing no one waiting for us, asked the hostess for a booth for four. The chatty brunette led us to a cozy spot next to a window where Mark and I sat side by side and pretended to look at the menu. Nervous energy crackled between us. Only five minutes passed before a cute couple slipped in, heads swiveling, obviously looking for someone. The woman sported a bulging third-trimester belly.

Mark and I caught the couple's eye, waved, and hurried over to meet them. My plans for a formal intro and an agenda-driven meeting went out the window as the four of us seemed propelled into a group hug. Releasing each other, we shared a nervous giggle and bustled to our table. At first, we exchanged stilted small talk; we noted the summer heat and discussed the Tigers' chances in the playoffs. After a minute or two, the conversation flowed more naturally.

Tim was talkative, which gave me a moment to observe and take note. He was round and jovial, with a shock of red hair, a wiry beard, and a boisterous laugh that put one at ease. When Tim shared his interests in history and digital music production, he and Mark connected instantly. It seemed Tim would be handling the lion's share of the conversation on behalf of Nita.

Nita was more reserved, though she bore an effortless Mona Lisa smile throughout the afternoon. With honey-blond hair pulled back into a bun and a graphic T-shirt sporting a horse with flowing mane, she struck me as a natural beauty.

When our meal arrived, Mark asked if he could pray, and Nita and Tim nodded their heads approvingly.

In between bites of quesadilla and Tim's chitchat, Nita softly shared her penchant for homemaking, including sewing and baking bread. She still dreamed of attending college one day.

She also described a scare she had experienced in her first trimester of pregnancy when she was helping out at her mother's hobby farm. She'd been feeding Shetland goats on a frigid winter day when one of the creatures attacked her. The ram had pummeled Nita directly in the belly with its horns, knocking her into the muddy snow. Her belly was mottled with bruises for weeks.

Months later, a doctor's examination (Wait, she hadn't gone to the doctor until months after the assault, despite her known pregnancy? I paused to marvel at her nonchalance) revealed a healthy baby in utero, apparently oblivious to the goat's attack. So here Nita sat, and obviously all was well.

She was radiant in her pregnancy, and, for the first time in five years, I felt not one iota of envy.

"I just know adoption is the right decision for us," she said, looking directly at me. That was the cherry on top of the joy bubbling up in me.

"Abortion was never an option for us," Nita said, "but we also couldn't just drop off the baby at some kind of orphanage."

For Nita, dropping off her child at an orphanage didn't gel with her morals. As an Infertile Myrtle, I was painfully aware that traditional orphanages in the vein of Little Orphan Annie didn't even exist in the U.S. anymore. If they had, I would have welcomed a baby home a long time ago, even if that required me to wait in the bushes outside the children's home, snatch a baby in the dead of night, and whisk it away in a Moses basket.

Ultimately, I was thankful I never resorted to kidnapping because it dawned on me as we munched on onion petals that the baby in Nita's belly was meant to be ours. I only hoped that Nita and Tim had had a similar epiphany; we were about to find out. Tim steered our conversation toward the reason we had gathered that day.

"Your profile caught my eye because you looked young, about our age," Tim explained. Apparently, the shot of Mark and I perched on the monkey bars at our local park had done the trick.

Nita found her initial impression of our profile a bit harder to articulate.

"There was just something about it. A sort of light," she said, as if light emanating from cardstock was a common phenomenon. "I grabbed yours from the pile right away and put it at the top of mine."

Nita and Tim had made an agreement when they walked in the doors of Adoption Associates to explore their options. They would individually look through the stack of profiles with which the agency had matched them and determine their top three couples; they didn't want to unduly influence each other. Once they'd finished this pre-selection process, they would share their picks with one another and make a decision.

As Tim told it, the pair was thrilled to discover that they'd each selected Mark and me as their first choice, their adoptive parent dream team. Mark and I were blown away that they'd reached such a clear consensus.

After this revelation, I was dizzy with anticipation. Did Tim's announcement mean what I thought it did? I'd shown up at this meeting hoping for the best but hadn't considered what an official match with a birth mom would feel like. Completing all of the initial adoption paperwork seemed miles away from expecting an actual son or daughter.

Suddenly, fear pulled me back to Earth. I regretted having put myself in this vulnerable position of hopeful adoptive mom. Despite the long line of disappointments we'd already swallowed on our journey to parenthood, there were still so many scary possibilities in the adoption process. I did not feel equipped to survive another disappointment.

Then I remembered the lessons that God had been teaching my stubborn head over the past five years: *You are not in control. You are not alone. I love you. I have good plans for you. Do not be afraid.*

I inhaled deeply and looked up from my reverie. Across the table, I directed a wobbly smile at the beautiful woman who held my hopes in her hands. Nita grinned back at me like the Cheshire Cat.

"We had an ultrasound," she said. "Do you want to know what this little bun-in-the-oven is?"

"Yes," Mark and I blurted in unison.

Nita was positively beaming with the promise of good news.

"You're having a girl."

A girl! Until now, my head had been filled with images of an androgynous cherub in cloth diapers, chubby and bald-headed. With Nita's report, a baby girl with long eyelashes and blond curls snapped into focus. A girl. Yes, of course. And we were going to be her parents.

I smiled at Nita. "That's wonderful!" I said and meant it. Mark agreed.

Tim gazed over at Nita again, grabbed her hand then glanced back at me. "Shelley told us that we get to put our name for the baby on the birth certificate," Tim said, "even though you guys can name her whatever you want."

"Yes, of course," Mark said, "that makes sense."

The digression seemed awkward, and I wondered why we had to discuss the topic of names right now, but Tim continued.

"We are going to name her Sara," he explained. "That's another reason we knew that you and Mark were the ones."

Mark and I, sitting side-by-side in the booth, turned our heads to look at each other. *How?* A lump formed in my throat, and the four of us shared a moment of silent awe, mulling over the holy workings that had brought us all together.

I grasped at the idea with finite understanding: Nita and Tim's unplanned pregnancy had been planned all along. The knowledge made me feel very small and very large at the same time. Mark and I had felt forgotten and left out of God's story for months upon years. Tim and Nita had likely wondered "Why us?", "Why now?" That day, the four of us sat staring at a coincidence of wants that made perfect sense in God's economy, the lines of our lives intersecting on the map of eternity to bring forth a new path.

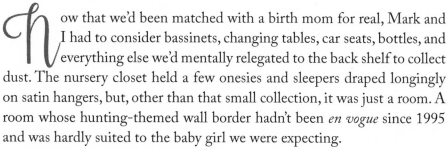

CHAPTER 10

Preparations

ow that we'd been matched with a birth mom for real, Mark and I had to consider bassinets, changing tables, car seats, bottles, and everything else we'd mentally relegated to the back shelf to collect dust. The nursery closet held a few onesies and sleepers draped longingly on satin hangers, but, other than that small collection, it was just a room. A room whose hunting-themed wall border hadn't been *en vogue* since 1995 and was hardly suited to the baby girl we were expecting.

As eager parents-to-be, Mark and I may have gone a little overboard in the decorating department. We decided on painting the room in a stripe pattern of green, white, and yellow, which required us to invest as much time in measuring lines and applying painter's tape as in brushing paint onto walls. We topped our design off with a whimsical wallpaper border depicting a portly moon surrounded by stars and cheerful insects.

The next step in our preparations involved attending a series of baby showers thrown in our honor. Anyone who was even remotely connected to Mark and me jumped at the chance to celebrate our long-awaited parenthood. Both sets of our school co-workers hosted parties. Our friends at the small United Methodist church we attended insisted on throwing us a shower in the basement, where generations of potlucks featuring meatloaf and tater tot casseroles still wafted from the walls.

And then there was the party to end all parties, the one hosted by my mom, her sister—my Aunt Judy—and my 80-year-old grandma. These faithful women were giddy to lead the charge away from five years of mourning into the next five of child rearing.

Mom had invited friends, family from both sides, and most of the congregation of Otsego United Methodist to my baby-palooza. As a result, we held the blowout in the OUMC's fellowship hall. If there is one thing Methodists know how to do, it is hospitality. The feasting, party games, and gift opening took hours, and I basked in the fellowship as I was initiated into the Mom Club.

During the gift opening, my sister-in-law, Lori, presented me with a goody bag of candles in "fresh linen" and "clean cotton" scents.

"Thanks Lori!" I exclaimed. "These will be perfect for relaxing in a hot bath!"

The women around me snorted and rolled their eyes good-naturedly.

"Um, you probably won't have time for baths anymore," Lori clarified. "Those candles are for masking the poop stench in the nursery."

Oops. I had definitely pictured myself in the Playtex baby bottle commercials, the mother in bathrobe rocking her pink-cheeked baby in the middle of the night, elated to croon lullabies at 3:00 a.m. Though I was a bit naïve to motherhood's grittier realities, I was ready for the poop and the spit up, and the lack of "me-time" (I had had my fill of me-time). These demands went hand in hand with caring for an infant, the one that was going to be mine.

I still held back a fraction of myself during these preparations and wondered daily, *What if this adoption falls through?* It seemed bad luck to prepare a nursery and start a layette when the birth parents could still renege. I behaved like an expectant mother, nine months along and sporting swollen ankles, but bringing home my baby depended entirely on Nita's labor pains and delivery, her decision to place the baby in my arms.

As the queen of doubters, I clung to my disbelief as a countermeasure, insurance in case of catastrophe. But I had to let go of my penchant for playing the devil's advocate. Faith led me beyond mere feeling into practice. I prayed without seeing, I spoke the truth of God's goodness before my belief grew roots. My trade-off of fear for faith was that illustrious "peace that passes all understanding," which is not merely a saying they slapped in the Bible but a real sense of calm that enters in when invited.

Though Mark and I chatted with Nita and Tim on the phone several times following our initial meeting, we only met in person one more time before our daughter's arrival. We gathered together in the picturesque courtyard at the Grill House in small-town Allegan, noshing paninis and kettle chips under the oaks.

Nita brought us an overflowing basket of her homemade bread, and we presented her with a pampering kit tricked out with lavender lotion, bath salts, and body wash, along with a devotional we hoped would bring peace and healing after the baby was born. Since I was clueless as to what to buy a birth father who was about to give us his baby, Tim would just have to share with Nita. They were clearly gaga over each other, so I imagined that a lavender bath with mutual back scrubbing was not so far-fetched.

Because I was desperate for this baby, I'd carefully considered the birth-parent gifts, engineering them to be generic, uplifting, and non-offensive. During this honeymoon period with Tim and Nita, I orchestrated every move to reinforce the image Mark and I had managed to portray since our first meeting, the notion that we were fit to parent their daughter. I even refused to have my unruly summer mane trimmed to my usual back-to-school bob in August, anxious that I'd spook the birth couple if I altered my look by a fraction.

After lunch, the four of us sat in the restaurant's canopied swing table and sipped lemonade as we rocked back and forth. Tim again did most of the talking, though Nita seemed always happy to be with us, content to listen and nod. The baby was due on October 10th, which was less than a month away, and Nita was in the uncomfortable stage of late pregnancy. Her feet were swollen, her bladder was the size of a thimble, and she felt like a small barge. In sum, Nita couldn't wait to finish labor and delivery. At her appointment three days earlier, the doctor had reported slight dilation and confirmed that the baby appeared healthy and ready to make her appearance straightaway.

I glanced back and forth between Nita and Tim as she recounted all the details of her appointment and couldn't help but notice Tim's devotion to her displayed through his reassuring presence. He was constantly playing with Nita's hair, placing his arm around her shoulder, or holding her hand. The look in his eyes communicated pure adoration and, to be honest, it gave me pause. How could he and Nita part with their baby in less than a month, I wondered, knowing they would be giving up the chance to parent a little human being whom they'd created together? There was much about their story I didn't understand, but I never questioned their sincerity. For reasons only Nita and Tim could fathom, they were following through with the adoption, convinced that Mark and I were their baby's very best chance at a life of opportunity and happiness.

Still, we hadn't yet discussed whether this would be an open adoption. Adoption has changed since the days when an unplanned pregnancy was shrouded in secrecy, documented in sealed records, and exclusively "closed," meaning that adopted children never met their birth parents. Since the 1980s, "open adoption" has become the buzz phrase, as all degrees of openness became legal, provided that birth parents and adoptive families agreed on the arrangements. In 2002, about 95% of domestic adoptions shared some level of openness.

Mark and I knew of couples who opted for entirely open adoptions in which birth mothers were woven into their children's adoptive families and hung out with them like an older sibling returning from college. In these situations, a birth mother might attend the child's birthday parties and sporting events or even join the adoptive family for vacations.

We also knew of arrangements in which birth parents and adoptive families had no contact. In our view, these two scenarios both represented extremes and our caseworker recommended that we strike a happy medium in the form of a semi-open adoption.

A semi-open agreement might involve sharing the birth experience (to the extent that the birth mother is comfortable doing so) and exchanging pictures and letters regularly through the child's fifth birthday and then annually until the child turns 18. This option sounded like something Mark and I could live with, but the ball was in Nita and Tim's court. We were hardly in a position to negotiate.

Until that day at the Grill House, the four of us had discussed everything *but* the subject of open adoption until, much to our relief, Tim brought it up naturally. He and Nita had already hashed out their ideas about openness and were confident in their plan, just as they were in their decision to place their baby with us.

"You two will be this baby's parents," Tim stated matter-of-factly, "and we don't want to interfere."

Tim looked back at Nita, and she smiled and nodded in agreement. Their firm vote of confidence shocked me, but it was comforting to know that Nita and Tim's ideas of adoption would allow us to pilot the plane as we parented this baby.

As much as we adored Nita and Tim—and we did—Mark and I didn't want to share our daughter—whether as a baby, toddler, child, or teen— with her birth parents. We knew the task of raising her would be enough of a challenge without adding another set of parents to the mix. I know that many birth parents and adoption professionals out there would disagree with what they perceive as our selfishness. Even so, the wisdom I had gleaned from books and articles about adoption, along with what my gut told me about parenting and kids, affirmed that semi-open was the best choice, not only for us but for our baby and for Nita and Tim as well.

Semi-open adoption offered closure and facilitated healing for everyone, whereas fully open arrangements could leave relational wounds to be torn open over and over again. Truth be told, Mark and I wanted this baby so badly that we would likely have agreed to any arrangement, but we were overjoyed when Nita and Tim shared our values and vision for openness.

After lunch, the four of us strolled out to the parking lot, where August's heat sent up waves from the asphalt. Mark and Tim lagged behind as I escorted a waddling Nita to her car. As she fiddled with her keys, she answered another question I'd been wondering about since our first meeting.

"If you're interested, we'd like you to be in the delivery room when the baby is born," Nita said softly.

I was astounded by the thought. *If I'm interested? Could there be any question?* At Nita's invitation, relief and anticipation flooded through me. She had opened the door that would allow me to participate in labor and delivery, rather than loiter in the hallway like the most awkward of spectators. More than that, Nita's graciousness meant that Mark and I could start parenting our baby not when a third party handed her over to us—all shined up and wrapped in a blanket—but the minute she slid out of the birth canal and into this world.

Our inability to conceive had stripped Mark and me of the wonder of experiencing pregnancy together. No positive home EPT or first trimester secrecy for us. We shared no blissful sighs at hearing our baby's heartbeat for the first time and had no opportunity to marvel together as we counted fingers and toes on a hazy ultrasound screen. Yet Nita's invitation into the delivery room would finally grant us that intoxicating sense of awe that accompanies each miracle. With tears, I thanked Nita and wrapped her and her belly in an awkward hug.

When we said our goodbyes moments later, Nita and Tim promised to call us at the first signs of labor. In 2002, constant contact through cell phones and social media was non-existent. Nita and Tim didn't have a landline. They owned one TracFone between them, and it was their only way to get in touch with us.

Three weeks later, when the due date passed without news from Nita and Tim, Mark and I jumped to the worst possible conclusion. Had they changed their minds?

The next day, we called Shelly, our caseworker, to find out if she'd heard any news. After touching base with Nita, Shelley assured us that all was well; the baby was just a little slow to make her appearance. Nita had a doctor's appointment the next day, and Shelley promised us an update. She called nearly every day after that as Nita moved eight and then nine days past her due date and required regular monitoring by the doctor.

Each day felt like sitting in DC's rush hour traffic. Mark and I questioned how Nita would handle the wait and whether having more time to think would cause her to re-evaluate her adoption choice. The hospital experience was the most precarious time for birth mothers and adoptive families. It represented a time when the idea of a baby became flesh and blood and resounding wail and a biological mother responded instinctively, both physically and emotionally.

Adoption Associate's workers were experts at preparing pregnant mothers for the birth experience and hospital stay afterward, but how much would Nita be able to ready herself for the baby placed in her arms within seconds of delivery? And how would Tim—who had never had a child—react when he saw his daughter's face for the first time?

Mark and I pondered all of these things as we waited and prayed. I'd love to say that we prayed for God's will; however, in our vulnerability we begged God to line his plans up with ours.

We prayed that Nita and Tim would stay resolute in their decision and have the vision to see past the emotional earthquake that was sure to come. We prayed to bring home a baby.

CHAPTER 11

For Unto Us

Mark and I got the call at 10:00 on a Saturday morning.

"Nita's been in labor since four-o-nine this morning," Tim stated calmly.

Four-o-nine…like the kitchen cleaner? I thought.

Then my reality check arrived. *Since four-o-nine this morning?* That was nearly six hours ago. And we had been rambling around the house like this was any ordinary Saturday, not the day our daughter would wriggle her way into the world!

Actually, that's not quite right. Mark and I had whiled away the morning debating whether to sit around waiting for that phone call or to go about our usual Saturday business of doing laundry, grocery shopping, and hanging pictures in the rooms of our new house. Between the two of us, we only had one cell phone, and Nita and Tim didn't have the number, so we resolved to play it safe. I would head to the store for milk and eggs, and Mark would hang by the landline in case there were any developments. Nita was 10 days overdue so the baby could—should—make her appearance at any time. We were just about to execute our Saturday plan when we got Tim's call.

"So we should meet you at the hospital?" I asked Tim.

In my mind, this wasn't an actual question. Speeding to the hospital is what pregnant women did when contractions started. Obviously.

But driving straight to the hospital's labor and delivery wing would've been too simple. Nita still sat at home, waiting until her contractions were only a few minutes apart. Tim instructed us to sit tight and wait. These contractions could be a false alarm.

Wait? Why did that word keep popping up? My gut told me I hadn't aced the lessons on patience thus far, so God, in his generosity, was handing me another opportunity for practice. Mark and I were closer than ever to having a baby, yet it was once again time to hurry up and wait.

We gritted our teeth and marked time. As each minute clicked by, we fought the urge to call Tim back or barrel to the hospital without his blessing. Meanwhile, an anthology of doubts spilled in between us. Would Tim call us back? With the baby on the way, would Nita and Tim change their minds about adoption? Would Mark and I make it to the hospital in time for the delivery? Did Tim mention how far apart Nita's contractions were?

An hour later, the phone rang.

"We're on our way to the hospital," Tim said. "See you soon."

For a first time father-to-be, he still sounded unruffled.

Mark and I, on the other hand, burst into a flurry of activity. After quick phone calls to our parents, we grabbed our overnight bags and a gift bag of goodies for Nita and scrambled out the door. As Mark backed out of our garage, I carefully checked off our supply list.

"Wait!" I shrieked.

We had forgotten the car seat. The one our baby would ride home in. I had only seconds for this thought to sink in: If all went well, Mark and I would bring our baby home tomorrow. The two of us were becoming three.

Shelley had warned us to have the infant car seat latched into the backseat and ready for action. The veteran caseworker had witnessed dozens of adoptive couples poised in hospital parking lots with babes in arms as she assisted with the complicated process of car seat installation. I grabbed the car seat from inside the garage and tossed it into the backseat. I hoped Mark's engineering prowess would allow for expeditious car seat placement before Shelley could witness our faux pas.

After I'd checked off my list and we'd hit the road, the initial panic subsided, only to be replaced by a trickier unease. In that 25-minute drive to the hospital, I had plenty of time to question the integrity of God's plan. Was my hope for this baby safe in his hands?

When Mark and I arrived at Allegan Community Hospital around noon, we found Nita and Tim in a private birthing room about twice the size of a regular hospital room. Nita sat up in bed, smiling serenely, with Tim at her side. The four of us hugged quickly, and Tim and Nita briefed us on her progress. Nita's water had broken, and she was four centimeters dilated, but her contractions were only uncomfortable, not yet painful. I'd been with two of my friends through their labors, and I knew by looking at Nita that the finish line was likely several hours away.

When the nurse, a spiky-haired blond in her mid-50s, clad in Pepto-Bismol pink scrubs, bustled in to monitor Nita's progress, Mark and I politely left the room only to pace in the hallway like caged tigers. We didn't want Nita to feel awkward, and we hadn't considered the fact that the nurses would be constantly checking and rechecking for progress in her dilation.

By 3:00 p.m., Nita was crying out every few minutes and thrashing from side to side in search of relief from the contractions. A crew of nurses ran in and out in a pink blur. As delighted as I was to be by Nita's side in the birthing room, I felt compelled to make sure she wasn't having second thoughts about inviting Mark and me into such an intimate event. It wasn't so long ago that I'd been in a similarly delicate position, with a gathering of strangers at the foot of my hospital bed for ultrasounds, follicle checks, embryo retrievals and transfers, and laparoscopic surgeries. To the extent that it was in my power, I wanted to spare Nita that discomfort.

Mark slumped in a chair against the wall to Nita's left, about five feet from the action. While Tim held Nita's right hand at her bedside, I hovered on the left, out of the nurses' way. After a wrenching contraction, I grabbed Nita's hand and looked into her sweet laboring face. Splotches of red darkened her cheeks and she was straining to catch her breath.

"Nita," I said, "I know that you wanted Mark and me in the delivery room with you, but if you're uncomfortable, we can wait in the hall, OK?"

Nita did not flinch. She squeezed my hand, and her eyes bore into mine.

"Sarah…" she said hoarsely between breaths, "this is *your* baby…and I want you right here."

My heart was bruised with tenderness for this brave woman, who I'd known for three short months, and the gift she offered me freely. Nita and I held tightly to each other's hands. My smile wobbled as I attempted two words, just now understanding their meaning. "Thank you."

Who but God could forge such a bond? Who but God could plant in a birth mother's heart such compassion for my emptiness?

Pushing Through

At 4:30 in the afternoon, Nita was fully dilated and enduring contractions up to 90 seconds long. Doctors and nurses passed in and out of the room at breakneck speed. Unfortunately, Nita had somehow missed the window for an epidural, so her doctor was only able to administer local anesthesia. Dispensing local anesthesia to a woman in labor is akin to giving a shot of whiskey to a patient having his leg amputated.

I had a sudden urge to berate the staff for not issuing us a heads-up on the epidural "window." It was a pretty vital task to let slip, and now Nita was on her back breathing heavily. She hadn't cursed at anyone yet, but I was about to.

The nurses were busy bringing towels and blankets and pushing buttons on a variety of contraptions, including one I recognized as a sort of bassinet with clear walls.

Suddenly, the spiky-haired nurse at Nita's feet announced that it was time to push. I held on to Nita's left hand, channeling my own strength into her as Tim held her right. The order to push propelled Mark to the edge of his seat. Lightheaded after the first push, I realized that I'd held my breath in concert with Nita and reminded myself to continue breathing. Nita needed me to stay upright by her side, not comatose on the hospital floor.

And where was the doctor? I posed this question emphatically to the room. Spiky Hair gently explained to me that the doctor would waltz in toward the end of this particular show. He was needed simply to catch the baby. I nodded to show that I'd gotten the message and would be causing the nurses no more trouble. It was hard to be an extra there in labor and delivery. I didn't know what to do with myself.

After 20 minutes of Nita's pushing, the nurses suddenly became interested in the fetal monitor. They huddled together, speaking in hushed voices that infuriated me. I made out something about calling the doctor. A nurse with a messy bun thrust open the door to the hall and bellowed for Dr. Savage; meanwhile, Spiky Hair instructed Nita *not* to push and helped her roll onto her left side. Adrenaline shot through me. I glanced back and forth at Tim and Mark for reassurance, but we were all clearly rattled.

Dr. Savage—who looked nothing like his name—blew in to examine Nita and the fetal monitor then exited abruptly, muttering something about a C-section.

Within seconds, a stocky woman who introduced herself as Nurse B burst through the same door to fill us in.

The baby's heart rate was dropping dangerously low with every push, she told us, and Nita was not making any progress. Dr. Savage suspected the cord was wrapped around the baby's neck, and he needed to perform a cesarean section. Nurse B reassured Nita the C-section was a routine procedure and the baby would be fine.

Nita pleaded with anyone who would listen, "I have to push!"

The women in pink turned to Nurse B, the major general of this operation, and awaited a response. Nurse B hesitated then gave the order.

"Let's give it a try."

As Nita rolled onto her back, Nurse B ordered Tim to hold Nita's right foot up to his chest so Nita could push against him. Messy Bun ordered me to act as a similar brace for Nita's left foot. Mark sprang up to take my place holding Nita's hand. I was now front and center for all of the dilated action, but Nita was beyond caring.

Another nurse rushed into the hall and called again for Dr. Savage.

Dr. Savage snagged a stool and spun it to the end of the bed, where he parked himself to survey the situation. Nita had already started pushing, and again the baby's plummeting heart rate sounded the alarm and triggered a flashing red screen. Why was Nita still here and not in surgery?

Dr. Savage leaned forward, hands outstretched. "OK, Nita, I need you to push again," he said softly.

Nita gritted her teeth through the push. Suddenly, I glimpsed a small circle that disappeared as the push ended, as if snapped back into the birth canal by a rubber band.

Dr. Savage sat back and planted his hands on his knees.

"Nita," he said, "the cord is wrapped around the baby's neck. I need you stop pushing until I tell you to, OK?"

Nita's eyes were squeezed shut, but she gave a weak nod.

The doctor took a deep breath and reached both hands into the birth canal. His head swiveled toward the ceiling as his arms and shoulders felt blindly for the umbilical cord.

Just then, Dr. Savage pulled his hands out and ordered, "Push!"

Nita sucked in a breath and curled forward, her fists clenched. The baby slid out. She was mottled and blue and still. I had stopped breathing.

Nurse B snipped the cord and swept the baby away, depositing her in the bassinet under a cluster of bright lights and surrounded by a med team. A flock of people in scrubs rubbed the baby's skin vigorously as Nurse B waved a plastic tube of oxygen under her nose. Within seconds a weak cry pierced the room.

I looked back at Nita. Her eyes were closed in exhaustion and relief. Tim had resumed his place by her side.

Like deer in headlights, Mark and I regarded each other across the bed with a sudden realization: We were free to get our first glimpse of the baby. Guilt pinched my gut as we left Nita and Tim to inch over to the bassinet. A couple of nurses were still perched around this baby girl, but we crept closer to count fingers and toes. She was calm and alert and had one tiny hand raised above her bright blue eyes in astute observation. Clearly, she was brilliant. Her skin was a lovely pink, and her head was covered in damp strawberry waves. The baby turned her head slowly toward Mark and me in recognition, it seemed, and I fell into her gaze.

My heart sped up as Nurse B, whom Mark and I later renamed "Man Hands," picked up our baby and began palming the kid like a basketball as she washed and dressed her, folded mitts over tiny fingers and pulled an impossibly small cap over her head.

When Nurse B finally handed the baby to Nita, everyone gathered around to "ooh" and "aah" until Mark and I excused ourselves to give Tim, Nita, and the baby some time alone.

We loitered awkwardly in the hallway wondering about our next move. How much time was enough before we could go back in and hold the baby? How would Nita handle our presence here now that the baby had arrived? Nita, Tim, Mark, and I had all agreed to a theoretical "hospital plan," but the plan was just a sketch. There's no way of knowing the "right" thing to do when a woman has just given birth to the baby you hope to take home. We'd have to wing it.

After about 15 minutes, Mark and I edged back into Nita's room, waiting for signs of her approval. The baby was still in her arms, and Nita beamed when she saw us, a tacit welcome. They had named her "Sara Marie," which would go on her birth certificate, along with Tim's and Nita's names as biological father and mother. "Marie" was Nita's middle name.

Even though Nita and Tim revealed the name choice at our first meeting, Mark told me later he was certain they'd picked the name "Sara" because they were so pleased with me as their baby's forever mom.

"My name is spelled with an 'h' on the end," I reminded him. Apparently, this one-letter variation only mattered to the Sarahs of the world.

As Mark, Tim, and Nita—with baby still in her arms—continued chatting, I skipped out to the restroom. Upon my return, I spied Mark comfortably seated in his chair against the wall and holding the baby. When he noticed me standing there, he sent a smug look that said, "Look who got to hold her first."

He's never going to let me forget this, I thought, but a few minutes later, Nurse B shook up a bottle of formula, cracked the seal, and handed it to me. At least I had won first feeding.

I glanced over at Nita to make sure she was OK with my providing the first meal. Her contented look signaled a green light, and I carefully took the baby from Mark's arms, aware somehow that this feeding was a test. I brushed the nipple back and forth gently across rosebud lips. Sara Marie quickly latched on and sucked heartily, the long journey into the world evidently having whetted her appetite.

"She probably won't eat much," Nurse B barked. "They're not usually too hungry this soon after delivery."

Heeding Nurse B's instruction, I stopped dutifully after each ounce to burp the baby, but she didn't quit eating until she had slurped down all four ounces. Despite her intense entrance, Sara Marie was the picture of health. Holding her securely against my chest, something inside me loosened. She was all I'd ever hoped for.

CHAPTER 12

Friends in High Places

*A*s the light faded outside, I realized that Mark and I hadn't yet set up a game plan. We had each brought an overnight bag but never considered where we would hang out for the evening. The birthing room offered space for Nita and Tim but not for an extra set of parents. As we discussed our dilemma outside the birthing room, a petite nurse we hadn't seen before motioned us down the hall. Apparently, the team of nurses who had cared for Nita all day had disclosed our piece of the story.

The nurse showed us to an empty room with a twin bed a few doors down and offered the space to us for the night. Mark and I were taken aback by the hospitality of this small-town staff who, remarkably, seemed to grasp the nuances behind adoption plans and had gone out of their way to send the message, "We've got your back."

We'd spent the day trying to position ourselves as loving adoptive parents rather than creepy kidnappers waiting to swoop in and swipe the baby from her unsuspecting birth mother.

The nurse's generosity had rolled out the welcome mat. We didn't have to steal through the hallways like thieves. We now had a place to rest our heads—like honored guests—and even bond with our baby. We were on the verge of becoming the family we'd spent years trying to build.

Mark and I slipped back into the room to clear our plans with Nita and Tim. Was it OK to bring the baby into our room to care for her for the night? I couldn't carry her in my womb, and I wouldn't be able to nurse her, but the fusing of our lives could begin right now. I could burst forth with the lullaby I'd held for her these five long years. Our daughter would know from day one how long she'd been waited for.

Nita and Tim nodded their heads at our request.

"You *should* spend some time together," Tim whispered. Then he turned his attention back to a drowsy Nita.

Mark and I tiptoed out, but once the door closed we rushed to the nurse's station asking, "Can we please, please, please have the baby in our room for the evening?"

After our new nurse friend, Kathy, got the nod from Tim and Nita, she led Mark and me into the nursery and over to the bassinet where our baby girl was swaddled and dozing peacefully. Kathy demonstrated how to unlock the brake and accompanied us down the hall as we wheeled the bulky contraption to our room. She informed us of what to expect in the next few hours, and Mark and I nodded along as her instruction drifted over our heads like clouds. My brain registered only one thought: *We have a baby!*

I thanked the nurse profusely for the room, her guidance, and the joy she quietly shared with us. An ear-to-ear grin was the last we saw of Kathy before the door closed with a click. And just like that, Mark and I were alone with our baby.

We padded over to the bassinet. I leaned forward and gently lifted the bundle to my chest. Mark hovered behind me, his five o'clock shadow grazing my cheek. We examined everything about her. The fontanel, where the rapid cadence of a heartbeat thrummed. The milia—small white bumps— that peppered her nose and chin. The pearly sheen of impossibly small fingernails.

Having finally shed our audience, I whispered her name—the name Mark and I had chosen for her.

"Adelaine Christina."

A sweet, old-fashioned name with a twist. Not Ade*laide* or Ade*line* as listed in baby name books, but Ad*elaine*. The last six letters formed a family name and reminded us of a beloved character from our favorite '90s sitcom, *Seinfeld*. Mark and I came up with it in our little house on Main Street when every Thursday night saw us planted on the couch for a line-up of "must-see TV." We were watching the "show about nothing" when we heard a wisecracking Jerry call Elaine, "Lainey." We agreed on the name instantly.

Mark and I sat down on the twin-sized bed as I cradled Lainey. She was beautiful, and I was her mama.

My heart swelled with the conviction that I could not love this baby more if I'd grown and given birth to her and that God loved me enough to say, "Wait," when I would have stupidly settled for "now."

I could have drowned in my gratitude.

I tore my eyes away from Lainey to check in with the new father. Mark's eyes were glassy, but his mouth barely held back a smirk.

"I held her first," he said, laughing.

And we wrapped our arms around each other and cried.

Doubt & Devotion

The night was long but with sleep punctuated every two hours by feedings and diaper changes. Mark insisted on sharing the load. We placed Lainey back into her bassinet after each feeding with our minds already set on establishing a schedule. I would've held Lainey every second but was keenly aware of my own need for sleep. Much like my dad, I had always required a full night's slumber and routinely curled up on the couch with a fuzzy blanket for glorious afternoon naps. Having a newborn at the seasoned age of 32 would undoubtedly put a dent in my nightly seven and a half hours of shuteye.

I snoozed lightly and lifted my head to check on Lainey every time she made a peep. I stretched my arm over the walls of her bassinet to feel her chest rise and fall. As soon as light seeped through the blinds of our solitary window, Mark and I wheeled Lainey, freshly changed and fed, into the birthing room with Nita and Tim and headed for breakfast at a mom-and-pop restaurant downtown. Nita would be discharged that day, and the two of them needed some private time with Lainey before they faced leaving without her.

Seated in a small booth over coffee and French toast, Mark and I processed the events of the last 24 hours. Our discussion took a turn for the worse as we once again entertained questions and doubts.

In the wee hours, with only Mark, Lainey, and me in our private room, we were decidedly a family. After we dropped Lainey off, however, Nita and Tim would hold their baby and have time to discuss the wisdom of their adoption decision. It was a delicate time and ripe for second thoughts.

Mark and I revisited Tim and Nita's reasoning. Their logic was focused on a desire to be a family of three—Tim, Nita, and Nita's 10-year-old daughter, Jessica—and a drive to pursue goals that would be difficult to chase while caring for a baby. They also didn't have the financial resources to care for Lainey. Tim worked a line job at a local factory, and Nita stayed home; though with Jessica in school full-time, Nita had the freedom to work or attend college classes.

There were other reasons for Nita and Tim's adoption plan that were murkier. Our caseworker, Shelley, had told us that Nita's childhood had been difficult. She had experienced some abuse, though Shelley didn't go into detail.

Nita's mother had visited the birthing room briefly the day before, and her presence plainly unnerved Nita. When the squat woman arrived, she barged in like she owned the place.

Observing Nita hooked up to an IV and monitors, her first words to her laboring daughter were, "They didn't have all this sh** when I was popping out puppies."

Nita cringed, and I fought the urge to act as a human shield against the woman's toxicity.

Tim's parents were another mystery, though infinitely pleasanter. Mark and I had met them in the waiting room along with Jessica. Tom and Cheryl were middle-aged, not unlike my parents, and we made polite conversation in attempts to convey our respect and admiration for their son's decision. Nita told us later that afternoon that Tim's parents had offered to help support the baby both financially and practically as a way of dissuading them from their adoption plan.

"But money has nothing to do with it," Nita insisted between contractions.

From Mark's and my perspective, Nita and Tim's rationale seemed anemic in a world where single moms were raising children on much less—less support, less love, less everything—than Nita and Tim currently possessed, but perhaps we were trying to wrap our human brains around a love that defied human logic. Nita and Tim's love for Lainey was unquestionable and their sacrifice anything but common. It brought to mind God's unconditional love for his people.

This love was of the ancient Greek "*agape*" variety, an unconditional and transcendent devotion that seeks to serve regardless of circumstances. It is the highest form of love, which lays down self for others, even when doing so is agonizingly painful. C.S. Lewis referred to *agape* as "gift love," and it is vibrantly expressed in the sacrificial love of Jesus' life on Earth and his death on a cross.

The world doesn't quite know what to make of *agape*. Mark and I certainly didn't understand the love we witnessed as a meek couple desiring more for their baby than they could provide entrusted her to us. We could only hope Nita and Tim's inexplicable love would hold firm when Nita was discharged from the hospital and the two of them went home with empty arms.

Moment of Truth

When Mark and I arrived back at the hospital, Nita sat in bed holding Lainey with Tim next to her. My heart did an unsettling jump, but we walked in and grabbed seats. Mark and I filled the two of them in on our eventful night, and they laughed at how eager we were to make sleep deprivation a permanent fixture.

"You might as well get used to it," Nita chuckled, "and get used to spit up and poopy diapers too."

She and Tim exchanged amused glances as she shifted her body uncomfortably.

"Will one of you take her?" she asked. "My arms are getting tired."

I held my arms out for the transfer. This was a very good sign. Nita was graciously putting us at ease and sending her message. *Nothing has changed. You're still this baby's mom and dad.*

Shortly afterward, Kathy poked her head in the door and encouraged Nita to dress and pack up. Nita seemed thrilled at her impending freedom. For a woman who'd given birth less than 24 hours earlier, she was quick to spring from her bed. I returned Lainey to the bassinet, and Mark and I left to give Nita some privacy.

So far, we'd only been able to share the news of Lainey's birth through covert phone calls. Usually, extended members of the adoptive family aren't able to be a part of the hospital experience, and Mark and I had been blessed to have the time to ourselves.

Now that Nita and Tim would be heading home, though, we could summon the troops. Lainey would stay for a few more hours for her hearing test, and Mark and I had signed up for a crash course in infant bathing with Nurse B. After Mark called his parents in Virginia, I got in touch with Mom, Dad, and Craiger.

We traipsed back down the hall toward the birthing room and found Nita dressed and fresh from the shower. She and Tim were waiting for us in front of the nurse's station with babe in arms.

"I've already lost five pounds!" Nita announced brightly.

"Congratulations!" Mark and I offered lamely as our eyes met. *Was this it?* We didn't have to wonder long.

Nita handed Lainey to me and wrapped her arms around me once more. I jostled to embrace Nita with my free arm as Lainey lay sandwiched between her first mother and her forever mom.

"Thank you," she murmured.

My mind was muddled, searching for the right words.

"We love you guys, Nita," I said. "I promise you we'll take good care of her."

We released each other, and Nita looked down at Lainey and then up at me with eyes glistening.

"I know," she said.

And then she was gone.

Tim quickly hugged both Mark and me, keeping his hands on our shoulders in his final blessing.

"The three of you are going to make a beautiful family," he told us, and with a fleeting glance at his daughter—our daughter—he followed Nita through the double doors. Mark and I watched through the glass panes until the two of them faded from sight.

I was torn in two. Half of me was giddy. The other half felt socked in the gut, winded from the grief Nita and Tim would slog through in the days ahead. In the past five years, I had become intimately acquainted with my own suffering; it was my second skin. I had always considered myself naturally empathetic, yet this stabbing sense of loss for another was new. The tension snapped inside me. I wanted this baby, and I wanted peace and wholeness for Nita and Tim; these goals seemed mutually exclusive. Nita and Tim's sacrifice was an elemental part of my joy, two sides of a coin that would produce the same outcome whether it landed heads or tails: one set of arms empty, one full.

As Mark and I stood in the whitewashed hallway, I sent up a song of mournful praise. *You give and take away.*

I could never be worthy of Nita and Tim's gift. I could, however, make a choice to be grateful every day. I could fill myself up with God's grace and mercy until it spilled over in the mothering of this baby and painted her world with the love that had brought her this long way. This unspoken conviction wasn't much in the way of offerings, but it was all I had.

Within 30 minutes, Mom and Dad, Craiger, and three-year-old Maddy bustled in through the same doors through which Nita and Tim had exited. Mom, not normally a germaphobe, had donned a surgical mask to protect Lainey from the sniffles. I took the minor gesture as a nod to the significance of Lainey's arrival and the lengths to which we would all go to love and protect her as a member of our family.

Mark and I were busy in the nursery when this bunch arrived. They peered through the window as we watched Man Hands flip a wailing Lainey from palm to palm while giving her a sponge bath in the hand-washing sink. Mark and I wouldn't be attempting a bath of this fashion any time soon. We had the American-Pediatrics-Association-approved infant tub at home, and we intended to use it. Very carefully.

Nurse B placed Lainey, naked and still squalling, down in her bassinet and handed me a diaper, onesie, socks, sleep sack, and beanie. It was go time.

Despite my practice the night before, I fumbled through the routine. Lainey's arms weren't bendy enough to thread them through the arm holes, plus I had Nurse B's scrupulous eyes watching my performance. Mark was on the other side of Lainey "helping," only not so much, since we were kind of out of sync. With Lainey finally dressed, Mark and I waltzed out into the hallway to show off our daughter to her adoring fans.

When the grandparents laid eyes on Lainey, they leaned in close and slipped promptly into baby talk.

"Look how pretty you are!" Mom burbled.

"Well, you were certainly worth the wait, weren't you?" Dad chimed in.

I squatted down to Maddy's level, and Craiger pointed out Lainey's small fingers and delicate head, cautioning his own toddler to be gentle. Wide-eyed, Maddy nodded and tentatively stroked Lainey's hair.

I looked up at my dad.

"Do you want to hold her?" I asked. Mom's sniffling and sneezing had landed her on the bench for the time being.

"Can I?" Dad said.

I handed Lainey over.

Mom observed from a safe distance and announced suddenly, "Her ears are so close to her head!"

We laughed at the strange compliment, and Mom explained she'd met many babies over the years whose ears had protruded too far from their noggins. But not Lainey. She was clearly an exceptional baby, smarter and more comely than the average infant.

After Mom and Dad had sufficient time to admire their new grand-daughter, and Mark and I had completed the necessary paperwork, we all walked out to the parking lot to say our goodbyes for the moment. A throng of people—family, friends, and neighbors—would be flocking to our house shortly to offer their congratulations and meet the newest Rollandini. When we arrived at our two-door Chevy Malibu, it was like the United Nations Assembly, everyone weighing in on how to buckle the baby safely in her car seat. Mark and I knew we'd followed the manual's instructions to a T, but Lainey's small form shrank into the cavernous space.

Mark chauffeured and I rode in the back seat next to Lainey watching her all the way home.

Bringing Home Baby

For adoptive parents, the trick about bringing a baby home from the hospital is that she's not really theirs yet, not until the court date. These eager new parents will feed, change, and sing their babies to sleep, but the budding relationship could be crushed in a moment if the birth mom decides she wants to give parenting a shot. Even when you know your child-rearing stint could be temporary, attempting to hold your affections back in self-protection is inconceivable. I know because I tried it.

Love is funny like that. You can't open your arms and safeguard your heart at the same time. There is love and there is fear; the two are incompatible. Perfect love, in fact, fiercely casts out fear into places unknown.

I had started loving Lainey on the day we chose adoption, and no amount of Satan-inspired anxiety was going to shake my devotion. I considered the possibility that Tim and Nita could change their minds, but this thought did not rein in my affection. I determined that if Lainey was only mine for a time, the love I had provided in her earliest days would be enough to sustain her for a lifetime.

I sang to Lainey every night. All the time, actually. I sang "Amazing Grace" as I rocked her in the soft yellow glider at the foot of her crib and grasped the meaning behind John Newton's words for the first time. Grace was the free and unmerited favor of God and I was the unworthy sinner onto whom his kindness spilled. For years, I had spewed anger and disbelief toward a loving Father, and yet here I sat with everything I thought he'd robbed me of—a child in my lap.

I sang "Hush Little Baby" and "Nighty Noodles" and "You are My Sunshine," putting my own spin on that folk melody. On my initial attempt, the song brought me to my knees.

You are my sunshine, my only sunshine. Of course this was true of Lainey. *You make me happy when skies are gray.* Yes, a thousand times over.

You'll never know, dear, how much I love you. Does any child know a mother's love until that child becomes a parent?

Please don't take my sunshine away. In the hush of this lullaby, I suddenly heard the screeching of brakes. My constant prayer was that Lainey would be ours forever, but I couldn't sing the last line of the chorus without tears plopping like raindrops onto the babe in my lap.

A lyrical revision was in order, at least until a few signatures in a courtroom made Lainey ours forever. I revamped the melancholy styling into a boldly hopeful phrase: *And I'll love you more every day.*

CHAPTER 13

Bitter & Sweet

I am what one might call the sensitive type. I don't have the sort of friends who toss around clever barbs in jest. Even small injustices have the power to rip a gash in my psyche: An ad from the Humane Society displaying wet-eyed dogs gazing at you from behind bars. A flippant comment from a student about the unbearable boredom he endures in my classroom. A news story about the homecoming king with Down syndrome. Even the road kill on my morning commute (that poor, poor raccoon!).

I wish I were kidding.

Despite my emotional frailty, however, I am not a crier. Instead, my sensitivity manifests itself in a stoic intensity and bouts of heavy sighing. I've often had students, family members, and friends grill me with the following charge:

"What's wrong?"

"What do you mean? There's nothing wrong."

"Really? Then what's up with the exaggerated sigh?"

About a month before Lainey was born, I discussed my predicament with my BFF, Reneé.

"Sometimes I feel like a good sob would do me some good," I moaned, "but the tears just won't come."

"Oh, I cry all the time," Reneé bragged, "like every day."

"Lucky." I pouted.

With an eight-hour road trip separating us, we abandon our to-do lists and our husbands for a weekly phone conference to address life's critical issues.

Though Reneé was never able to break down the barriers in my tear ducts, Lainey was. In the weeks after we brought her home, my disability seemed to resolve itself. I could be changing a poopy diaper when the sight of Lainey's chubby smile pricked tears. Mercy Me's *Word of God Speak* would float from the clock radio in the kitchen while I was sweeping up dust bunnies and force me to collapse on the laminate floor. While I was reading my nightly devotional, the reality of God's generosity would swallow the doubt that had taken root over our five-year wait and replace it with sobs of gratitude.

It appeared that the tears I had mostly kept at bay for three decades had been stored up for my maiden voyage into motherhood. I held a snoozing Lainey one golden October day, settled in the window seat in our front room. As I read an adoption poem in an infertility newsletter, its poignant words defied worldly logic. Was the connection between Lainey and me not more of a miracle because of its unlikelihood? Was she not more of a gift because of the strings God must have pulled to bring us together? Piddly human hoop-jumping could not have resulted in me mothering this child. I bawled into Lainey's sweaty head that day, knowing full well the bounty that lay sleeping in my arms.

During my wait, girlfriends, aunts, and sisters-in-law waxed on about God's so-called plans.

"The Lord must have something very special for you," my friend Anna trilled.

But I never could swallow the bitter pill of waiting, of not being the captain of my own ship. Christianese sometimes flows easily from believers who have yet to face their own crises.

For me, believing had always depended heavily on seeing. I recognize my Doubting Thomas ways. On the good days of waiting for God to act—when he and I were on speaking terms—I still wasn't patient for his cosmic plans if he overlooked my desires in the equation. Since I knew what was best, I had rejected his schemes unequivocally throughout our grappling with infertility.

I had pushed my body through synthetic hormones and medical procedures and pushed my marriage to the brink. Seeking medical treatment for our infertility was not inherently sinful, but I had missed the mark when I stubbornly refused to seek God's wisdom first.

Now here I was, with Lainey, staring his divine purpose in the face.

People had God's desires all wrong about "closing a door to open a window." This aphorism, which seemed so apropos when Mark and I were on hold for a baby, revealed itself as an utter falsehood after we brought Lainey home. What fool would choose a window over a door anyway?

In Revelation 21: 5, John speaks of God making everything new and my jubilation in my adopted child had indeed broken new ground. Lainey was my constant reminder. Of course, God knew that we humans would be a forgetful lot so he even advised us to write down his promise. *This situation you think you can't live with? This thing you think you'll die without? I am making it, making you—making everything—new.* Jot it on a sticky note. Post it on your fridge and use it as your screensaver. Tie a string around your finger or snap a rubber band around your wrist if you must. *He is making all things new.*

The ruler of the universe did not need my cooperation or my feeble belief to accomplish his purpose for the Rollandini clan. As I held Lainey in our front windowsill, I understood that he had crushed my doubts and fulfilled my longing in a show of his power and dependability. In my infertility, God offered me no consolation prizes. Lainey was not his Plan B: She was nothing less than the good and perfect gift that comes only from the father of lights.

By the end of October, though, my spontaneous weeping continued with such frequency that I began to grow suspicious. I mean, sure, I was a new mother, but I could barely look at Lainey without blubbering all over her lacy sleepers (courtesy of all those baby showers).

One day, I was flipping through the calendar in our kitchen to find the date of Lainey's next doctor's appointment when I noticed a red X in mid-September, the one marking what should have been my monthly curse.

My brain was so addled by the placement of that red X that I had to pull a pad of paper out of the junk drawer to do some calculations. I checked and rechecked my math, even using my fingers as a failsafe accounting method.

(Have I mentioned that math is not my strong suit?) I shook my head at the improbability of my findings and reminded myself that my missed period was probably caused by the stressors of the past month—a new baby, uncertainties about court dates, a major sleep deficit, etc. But there was no way around it: After 18 years of maddening regularity, I was late.

I waited until the next day to drive to Timbuktu to buy a pregnancy test. I couldn't risk neighbors spotting me purchasing the contraband in a nearby pharmacy and sparking a wildfire of rumors about the poor infertile lady who was finally going to have "her own" baby. And right after she adopted! If one believes such an invasion of privacy is far-fetched, one hasn't made a trip to their friendly small-town pharmacy lately.

Frugal by nature, and by necessity because of debt incurred during our crawl to parenthood, I resented the idea of forking over cash for a pregnancy test that would surely turn out to be negative. Still, I had to get to the bottom of my mysterious mood swings and weepy disposition. I wondered if, instead of a pregnancy test, a prescription for Prozac might be in order.

Arriving home after my top-secret mission, I deposited Lainey in her crib for a nap and rambled into the bathroom to pee on the dreaded stick. I had downed plenty of water in the hour before in preparation. As I doused the stick with my sample, I pondered how many of these tests I had completed in the last five years. Too many, that's for sure. My addiction to at-home pregnancy tests had taken hold shortly after Mark and I started trying to conceive and way before the idea of infertility had sprouted in my mind. I tested within a few days of having sex, sure that our pregnancy would be so robust that it would register long before a missed period.

I'd broken my EPT habit somewhere between our first failed IUI attempt and our foray into IVF. The meds required for *in vitro* fertilization would have skewed the results anyway. Having kicked the habit cold turkey, I'd kept a spotless record ever since. Until now.

I lifted the wand from the recesses of the toilet and stared down at it with disdain. Reaching for the vanity, I laid the stick down on a tissue on the green laminate counter. After cleaning up, I shuffled back to the kitchen, set the stove timer for five minutes, and went to work washing the collection of baby bottles that had piled up with Lainey's frequent feedings.

When the timer beeped, I kept on working. I finished up washing, dried the dishes completely, and put them away to prove that the EPT stick was not the boss of me. I then scanned the kitchen for something more to do, something that would delay the inevitable. I already knew what that old stick would say and hated revisiting the disappointment I had banished nearly a year ago. It sickened me to have the joy of mothering Lainey overshadowed by my old nemesis.

My clean kitchen counter and empty sink stared back at me blankly with the message, "There's nothing more for you to do here." Resigned, I sighed and marched back to the bathroom. Picking up the plastic stick, I ran my eyes over its oval window, snorted, and hurled it into the trash. Two lines. The stick had always been a disappointment. What had I expected?

I left the bathroom in a huff, shaking my head at my own stupidity at chucking another 20 bucks down the drain and headed for the laundry room. Maybe I could salvage the afternoon by folding several piles of clean clothes before Lainey woke up.

Then an itching sensation tickled the back of my brain. I raced back to the bathroom and reached into the collection of cotton balls, crumpled tissues, and discarded dental floss to retrieve the stick I had tossed out a minute earlier. Bringing the wand up to the light, I squinted at the pink lines, struggling to discern their meaning. Lines. Two pink lines, not one.

I reached into the trash again and snagged the directions for the test, focusing on the informative pictures under the words "How to Read Your Test." The pictures made it easy, though I still glanced back and forth between the two—directions in my left hand, wand in my right—in disbelief. I finally slapped the directions down flat on the countertop and placed the stick on top of the creased paper, directly below its match. Two dark, unmistakable pink lines in the diagram and on the stick left no room for ambiguity, and the words above the picture sealed the deal. *Your results: pregnant.*

Dumbfounded, I called Mark at work, knowing he would probably be too busy teaching a class full of middle schoolers to take a phone call. Somehow I'd gotten lucky. It was his free period, and the office secretary quickly patched me through.

"Hey, what's up?" Mark greeted me in his deep baritone.

"You're not going to believe it," I blurted, "I'm pregnant!"

After a few seconds of silence, he responded with an unruffled, "Really? Cool…"

Mark has a frustrating tendency to underreact to shocking news. I'm sure this has something to do with the jarring disappointments we encountered in our eight years of marriage, but it is also his natural bent. And yes, his pragmatism is a counterbalance to my flighty tendencies, but come on! This was a pregnancy! Fertilization between my egg and Mark's sperm without any medical intervention or the swipe of a credit card. Wasn't this excellent news?

"Yeah, it's great," Mark stated unconvincingly. "You'd better call Doctor Dodds and find out what we're supposed to do next."

Oh yeah…Dr. Dodds. Because no matter how this pregnancy came about, my medical history made it anything but routine.

Fragments of our conversations bounced around in my head, terms like "high risk" and "increased chance of ectopic pregnancy." I guess I couldn't just roll merrily along waiting for my belly to pop out like so many joyfully clueless mothers spent their first trimester. I had to throw myself at the mercy of a tribunal of experts, hoping for them to give me the all-clear.

Mark and I signed off, and I quickly dialed Dr. Dodds's office. (I still knew the number by heart.) The nurse on the other end listened kindly, if not enthusiastically, and instructed me to make haste to the nearest lab for a blood test confirmation. Dr. Dodds's office would get back to me the next day.

The Test

When Mark arrived home from work, I plopped Lainey into his arms and gave him the rundown on her next feeding time and last poopy diaper. I had to race to the lab for my blood test because I am a straight-A patient and follow directions religiously. I figured this fastidious attention to doctor's orders should pay off somewhere down the line.

The nurse called the next morning as Lainey and I were lazily cuddling in my queen-sized bed.

"Congratulations!" she chirped. "You're pregnant!"

I wondered how many times the RNs at Dr. Dodds's office had been able to deliver this news to patients who'd called it quits on infertility treatment.

"Really?" I asked, gazing down at Lainey's long lashes. My daughter seemed to be hanging on my every word. "You're sure? Is there any chance the blood test could be wrong?"

"Nope," she replied. I could hear her smile. "Your HCG levels look great; you are definitely pregnant!"

I had about two seconds to rejoice before the nurse continued, "We need you to come into the office for an early ultrasound in the next few days because of your history of ectopic pregnancy."

And there it was, the mushroom cloud rising up from the middle of my field of wildflowers.

Lainey started to fuss. Time for a bottle.

"Would you like me to connect you with scheduling to make that appointment?" the nurse continued.

"Sure," I answered, "thanks."

What I wanted to say was, "Sorry, I can't make it. I'm a little busy right now."

Ultrasound Anxiety

Mark and I hadn't spilled the beans about our positive pregnancy test, hoping to spare our loved ones any disappointment until we had irrefutable evidence.

We marched into the ultrasound room with Lainey in tow to face the dreaded task together. It had been over a year since we'd seen Dr. Dodds for our last frozen transfer, and, while he scrubbed up, I caught him up on the latest.

We had Lainey, all fresh and smelling of newborn, right there in her car seat to show off. *See! After everything, we have a baby now!* Dr. Dodds demonstrated the appropriate level of awe and admiration for Lainey, tickling her cheek and even engaging in a little baby talk. Like Dr. Young and the majority of staff at the clinic, Dr. Dodds had an impeccable bedside manner. He had always taken time to look me in the eyes, not just treat my broken parts.

After we broke the ice, I lay back on the table and took a deep breath, preparing myself for the all-too-familiar procedure.

"Remember what happened the last time we were here?" I pressed Dr. Dodds.

The last time had marked the beginning of my summer spent in and out of the hospital.

Dr. Dodds nodded solemnly.

"Let's just see what's going on in here," he said as he inserted the ultrasound wand.

Dr. Dodds twisted the knobs and tilted the screen then maneuvered the probe to achieve optimal positioning. Again I tried to discern the images on the screen, but the light and shadows held zero meaning.

A minute, then two, went by as Mark and I made eye contact, him raising his eyebrows, me shaking my head. The silent waiting made my head spin.

"Well," I ventured, "what's the verdict?"

Dr. Dodds's hopeful face remained glued to the screen as he continued jostling the probe in what seemed to be a search-and-rescue mission.

Finally, he pulled out the probe and raised somber eyes to meet mine.

"I'm sorry," he muttered softly, "there's no heartbeat."

The second hand on the wall clock clicked, and the murmur of nurses' voices floated by in the hall.

"Another tubal?" I asked, business-like. I was not going to cry.

"No," Dr. Dodds replied, "the baby is in your uterus. I can see the sac, but it's collapsing. You're going to miscarry. I'm so sorry."

I nodded my head deliberately, trying to absorb his words, which held both bad news and good.

This baby would not make it, but we had achieved a pregnancy on our own, an idea we had long ago abandoned. Doctor Dodds trudged out, I threw my clothes on, and Mark and I hugged as Lainey gazed up at us from her car seat on the floor. This room was full of sad memories of the babies we'd lost, but now it also held the comfort of the one we had found along the way.

Afterward, we headed down the hall to Dr. Dodds's office for a quick consultation, where he told us what to expect over the next week. My body knew what to do and would be ridding itself of this baby. The miscarriage would feel like a heavier than normal period with cramping and an excess of blood, only our child would be coming out with it.

The good news came as Dr. Dodds escorted us to the emergency exit so we could be spared a tramp through the waiting room.

"What does this mean?" we asked him. "What happens now?"

"It means you can get pregnant," he stated matter-of-factly, "and that the embryo can make it all the way to the uterus, where it's supposed to be."

And the good doctor's last bit of advice for Mark and me as we stepped out into the sunlight: "Make hay while the sun's shining."

The Futility of Why

After a week, there was no sign of a period, so I was scheduled for a D&C. For those in the fortunate position of being unfamiliar with miscarriage lingo, D&C stands for dilation and curettage and is a brief surgical procedure in which the doctor dilates the cervix and scrapes the uterine lining, or, in my case, scrapes out a failed pregnancy that refuses to evacuate itself.

Since Mark had already taken a chunk of time off after Lainey's birth, I recruited my mom to accompany me. I would be too drugged up to drive home afterward and since Lainey was, at less than a month old, too young to be left with a sitter, she came along as well. A newborn in a car seat is adaptable to pretty much any situation, and Lainey was my talisman. When all was said and done, I was still this adorable girl's mama.

The procedure was uneventful, unless you count the fact that I dozed off before the surgery in a cozy room with Dr. Dodds and assistant nurse Heidi hovering over me and came to in a frigid room clattering with the voices of clinic staff. Along with my mother, nurses and doctors stood around the bed calling my name and patting/slapping/shaking me into consciousness.

"What happened?" I asked woozily. I felt like I might just hurl on Dr. Dodds's blinding white coat.

"She's back," buzzed a voice from the foot of my bed.

"She's OK," said another from behind me.

My mom's face came into view to my right. "How are you feeling, honey?" she asked.

I knew I was a long-time patient at the clinic, but what was up with the VIP care? Did our health insurance have a platinum plan for frequent fliers?

Both Dr. Young and Dr. Dodds suddenly appeared, peering at me with relieved expressions.

Apparently, I had experienced a "vasovagal attack" during the D&C, during which my heart rate had suddenly dropped to an alarming level. A vasovagal attack, I learned later, involves slowing of the heart, reduced blood pressure, and reduced blood circulation to the head, which decreases oxygen supply to the brain and can lead to fainting or convulsions.

Dr. Dodds had a much more succinct way of putting it. "Your cervix does not like to be messed with," he reported.

I begged to differ. In the past five years, my cervix had been messed with quite a lot and—up until then—had had a nearly spotless record, thank you very much.

After my blood oxygen returned to normal and I proved I could sit up and even stand without fainting, Dr. Dodds cleared me to leave. Mom chauffeured Lainey and me home and got us safely in the house before hugging us goodbye. Mark would be home in half an hour.

Within minutes, I was cramping and bleeding heavily, a full-blown miscarriage. I placed Lainey in her car seat in the middle of our bed before stumbling to the bathroom. I could see her from my perch on the toilet.

"I'm sorry," I cried out to her as I doubled over and tears coursed down my cheeks.

Lainey was happily oblivious to the trauma, but I felt like I had betrayed her, momentarily stealing the affection and delight she deserved.

My brain once again grasped for answers. Why had God chosen to allow this seemingly random miscarriage when he had the full power to protect me from it? And why at the moment when I had finally laid hold of the joy of being a mother? Was God really in control? I continued to hurl my whys at God, knowing he could handle my disillusionment, though asking "why" only wrecked my sense of peace.

I had learned in therapy that doubt's nemesis is trust. We lust after answers while God calls us to rely on him in our mess. Determined to take hold of my heavenly Father's promise to work all things for good, I labored to quash my incessant self-reliance. And Lainey was an ever-present reminder of God's affinity for breathing beauty into ashes.

Forever Family

A month later, on December 19, 2002, Mark and I held hands in the small wallpapered office at Adoption Associates with Rich, the agency's executive director. With Christmas less than a week away, we prattled on about our shopping lists and the weather forecast as I tried to breathe deeply.

It was 11:15 a.m., and Nita and Tim were currently in a county courtroom, answering the judge's short list of monumental questions and signing the consent forms that would make Lainey our forever daughter. We awaited one simple phone call from Shelly, our caseworker, to make our parenthood indelible. Aside from a brief period when Nita had experienced nightmares of crying babies and been diagnosed with postpartum depression, the last several weeks had been uneventful. We'd had no indication that Nita and Tim would change their minds about their adoption plan, but I started when the phone rang.

Rich picked up the receiver from his desk.

"Adoption Associates, this is Rich," he said, fiddling with his striped tie.

"Uh-huh." Rich looked up and gave us the thumbs up sign. I still wasn't ready to jump up and down.

"OK, thanks Shelly. You too. Bye."

Rich smiled as he placed the phone back in the receiver.

"Congratulations!" he said. "Nita and Tim signed the papers. You are officially Lainey's parents."

Mark grabbed me, and I squeezed my eyes shut to cork the tears. I'd had enough crying.

We still had a few home visits to go before the state of Michigan would recognize Lainey as a permanent part of our family, but these were mostly a technicality. The last appointments would affirm that our home was safe and that Lainey was being well cared for, a piece of cake compared to the paperwork and interviews through which we had persevered to bring her home in the first place. No caseworker in the world would have argued that we didn't pass parenting muster.

About a year later, while Lainey was taking her first toddling steps, we completed our home study and finalized her adoption. That evening, we held a little celebration at our house with my parents. After a dinner of Lainey's favorite, sweet potatoes, we read to her from *Tell Me Again about the Night I Was Born*. While our narrative was quite different from the one Jamie Lee Curtis shares, placing this book in Lainey's chubby hands was one small way Mark and I were making adoption a part of our everyday lives. We hoped to send a clear message to our daughter that her adoption story was an open book from which we were committed to sharing freely.

That night, the A-word had suddenly become a wondrous thread that sewed us together. Not just in our eyes, but legally and in every other way that mattered, Lainey was ours and we were hers. And this was only the beginning.

CHAPTER 14

Flying Solo

There is a picture forever seared in my mind of a toddler Lainey in pigtails adorned in the unlikely ensemble of a lacy white undershirt, barber's pole striped tights and chunky black boots—pants were unnecessary. She is skipping in circles around our deck with bare March trees in the background, singing, dancing, and striking poses, rather ungracefully, I might add, on account of the combat boot weighing down each wee foot.

I savored Lainey's unfolding of personality and hungered for more moments like this. Mothering, at its core, means partnering with God in shaping a soul; even on the tough days, when I was covered with vomit or shattered by the constant physical demands, I sensed that God was quietly, gloriously calling out my child's unique purpose. And I lifted my face to the sky in gratitude.

In January, just a few months after Lainey turned one and her adoption was finalized, Mark and I again began the process of adopting. We didn't know how long the second time around would take and figured it couldn't hurt to get our paperwork and home study in order to get a jump on that waiting game. Since the adoption process was now familiar and our home study only needed tweaking, we breezed through appointments, signed checks, and finished off paperwork at lightning speed.

We officially began our wait for baby number two in April. One drizzly morning on my 30-mile commute to work, I heard a radio program about a mom who had started praying for her young children's future spouses years before they would even start dating. I latched on to this idea immediately. Rather than squandering the wait for our child, I could do something practical by praying for his or her birth mother. I didn't even know if our baby had been conceived yet, but I prayed for our birth mom's emotional and physical health and that God would hold her in the palm of his hand and bring us together at the proper time.

Since I tended to be a bit of a Thomas, this prayer was a stretch for me. Would my intercession for a woman I'd not yet met make any difference? Even as I reminded myself that our second child's birth mother would be a significant part of our lives one day, I wondered if God had time for this kind of request. I prayed, and I doubted.

In September, Mark and I had been waiting six months with no word from Adoption Associates and had returned to school after summer vacation. Lainey was almost two, and we'd spent June, July, and August visiting the playground at our local park, camping near Lake Michigan, and splashing in Mom and Dad's pool. We never tired of showing Lainey off to bystanders or trotting after her as she hunted for ladybugs.

One day after school, I sat exhausted in my classroom when Josh, a recent graduate, lumbered in for a visit. This is the great paradox of the high school student: While in school, they spend hours sprawled lazily across their desks complaining of boredom, yet, months after graduation, these same scholars return to their alma maters like pilgrims to the holy land.

I had loads of planning to do and was secretly thinking, *I really don't have time for this, kid,* but I popped out of my chair to greet him anyway.

"What's up?" I exclaimed, giving Josh a quick hug.

Josh had been in my seminar class—a glorified study hall—since freshman year and stayed in the course until graduation, so we'd had four years to get to know one another. The growth that takes place in teenagers between freshman year and the pomp and circumstance of graduation is extraordinary. Josh had started as a gangly, awkward kid and was now a tall, self-possessed young man, well spoken, direct, and armed with a dry wit.

When I asked Josh to catch me up on the latest, he told me he was delivering pizzas full-time and attending community college to study law enforcement. He had also recently broken up with his girlfriend, Amy.

"What happened?" I asked, expecting him to borrow from the library of typical break-up narratives. *We fought too much. We're too young to be tied down. Our colleges are too far apart.*

Instead, Josh shuffled from side to side before clearing his throat and answering uncomfortably.

"Well, she's pregnant."

"Oh," I replied, eyebrows raised.

All of the social niceties tumbled through my mind, but—since this was Josh, my student of four years—I ditched the bilge for a more direct approach.

"Are you the father?" I asked.

"No!" he blurted angrily. "She's in the army stationed over in Germany. Some guy over there got her pregnant."

Josh was a sensitive kid, and I'd seen him fall head over heels a number of times during high school, but this seemed rough. As I cringed and muttered an "I'm sorry," a light bulb clicked on in my head. What I had originally viewed as an interruption in the day's busy schedule suddenly registered as more than a random visit.

Do I dare? I thought.

"Josh," I ventured, "did you know that my husband and I are officially waiting to adopt again?"

"No," he replied, "that's cool."

Josh had not yet connected the dots, so I rushed to complete the picture for him.

"Umm, your ex-girlfriend—Amy—does she have a plan for the baby?"

My absurd question sat like an elephant between us, and I was embarrassed at my brashness. In 2007, most pregnant teens did not have adoption on their minds. Still, something nudged me on through the discomfort.

"You know, is Amy going to parent the baby or…" I continued.

"Oh, yeah," Josh replied, sheepishly. "She wants to put the baby up for adoption."

I wish I could say that I took the time to correct Josh on his ignorance about adoption language ("Put up for adoption"? Ahem, we are not talking about a livestock auction here), but I was too shocked that news of a birth mom with an adoption plan had just dropped into my lap.

"Is Amy working with an agency? Has she picked parents for the baby yet?" I asked, trying to stifle my excitement.

Then I saw the light bulb turn on in Josh's head and light up his face.

"No, I don't think she has...I could give her your number!" he proposed.

Way to get on board, Josh.

"Would you?" I implored, probably not sounding at all desperate. "I mean maybe Amy's already figured everything out, but it couldn't hurt, right?"

Grinning, Josh nodded.

"Sure, Mrs. Rollo!" he agreed. "I can't wait to tell Amy all about you. You've always been one of my favorite teachers!"

I could have kissed Josh on both stubbly cheeks just then but wanted to avoid being arrested for assault since I had a baby at home and, just possibly, one on the way.

And that is the story of how one of my all-time-favorite students became the most important reference of my life.

Amy called that very evening (I was growing more impressed with Josh by the minute).

When I dashed into the bedroom to grab the phone, I felt like I was in the middle of an intense hot flash.

"You've been teaching and ministering to teens for the last ten years," I reminded myself. "You should have no problem relating to this 19-year-old girl in a tough spot."

I sat down on the edge of our bed, drank in the calming blue walls, and picked up the phone.

"Hello?" I said.

"Hi," came a soft, low voice from the other end. "This is Amy? Josh gave me your number?"

Where there should have been a period, each sentence lilted up like a question. Amy sounded hesitant and lost, and my compassion bloomed immediately. How many young adults were brave enough to make a cold call to anyone, much less an adult who might be the future parent of her unborn child? Amy had won my admiration and respect right out of the gate.

"Hi, Amy!" I piped. "I've been looking forward to talking with you!"

My salesy tone took me aback. I really needed to take it down a notch.

The words—and exclamation points—were real, but the hyperventilation had transformed my alto into a screechy soprano. Amy didn't seem to notice.

"Yeah, me too," she answered warmly.

Our conversation started a bit slowly, so I quickly accepted the role of counselor and directed Amy to catch me up on her story. I could almost hear her wheels turning on the other end as I waited for answers to my flood of questions.

My Q&A was aimed at getting to know Amy as a person and finding out where she was in the adoption process. I hoped that Mark and I were a match for Amy, but as I listened to her story, I found myself acting more like a mentor than potential adoptive mom. At 19, Amy was so much like many of my students. She came from a broken home and was stuck sharing a cramped bedroom with her elementary-age brother in the small home of her combative mother and stepfather.

Amy had joined the army with hopes of traveling the world and getting a college education, but, without a support network, she instead found herself pregnant and medically discharged. She was disillusioned with how quickly she had been forced to forfeit her dreams.

"I want my baby to have a mom and a dad," Amy said decisively. "I'm living with my mom, I don't have a job, and I know that I can't give this baby what she needs."

And there it was. Another girl.

"You know it's a girl?" I asked casually, not knowing if my relationship with Amy would live past this phone call. It seemed like a natural question, not too prying or presumptuous.

"Yes," she said, "I had an ultrasound over in Germany, and they were pretty sure it was a girl."

I heard Mark and Lainey giggling outside my closed door and imagined my two-year-old holding her baby sister carefully, head propped on the checkered pillow at the end of our living room couch.

"So," Amy cut in, "do you think you could come over here some time so we could meet?"

Well, this was new. Come over? To the birth mom's house? Would this be a supervised visit or had this phone call just landed me in unfamiliar territory without the guidance of an adoption agency?

I barreled ahead. "Sure, I could do that. How about tomorrow night?"

Apparently, I was now making everything up as I went along.

According to Amy, the following night was perfect. She gave me directions to her house, just 25 minutes away, and we said goodbye until then.

I perched on our bed, considering my decision to forge such an intimate connection with Amy and whether the visit to her house the following night was a good idea. I wasn't sure I was ready to know where Amy lived or to meet an expectant mother without an adoption professional. Wasn't there some forbidden line between birth mom and adoptive, and wasn't I in danger of crossing it?

Still, when I thought about Amy, I noticed that tenderness towards her had replaced my nervousness. Perhaps I could ease her through the adoption process in some small way as Amy made it possible for me to become a mother of two.

Not one to act rashly, I had always sought balance in my walk with God, a happy medium between blind faith and common sense. I didn't know if saying yes to an unscripted meeting with Amy had upset this equilibrium, but the words of Isaiah 41:13 sprang to mind. *"For I am the Lord your God, who takes hold of your right hand and says to you, 'Do not fear; I will help you.'"*

After all I had seen God accomplish, why did I continue to fancy myself the CEO of a little company called "My Life"? I wasn't in charge now and never had been, and—caseworker or no caseworker—I certainly wouldn't be flying solo when I met Amy the next evening.

CHAPTER 15

Red Flags

*T*here's no doubt that seeing God's providence all over Lainey's adoption had made me brave again. I no longer cowered in a corner waiting for the worst but flung open the door to welcome our next adventure. I knew that whatever snags we encountered in our second adoption, the grand finale would wipe out the angst along the way.

By the time I landed on an appropriate outfit for my first meeting with Amy, however, our bedroom floor was littered with shirts, pants, belts, and shoes. Normally, getting dressed didn't involve such a fashion frenzy, but there were no magazine articles entitled *Five Perfect Outfits to Woo a Birth Mom*, and Pinterest hadn't been invented yet. So, at 34, I suffered in isolation, doomed to rely on my own declining fashion sense. I finally pulled on a pair of jeans and a sweater, hoping to strike a balance between youthful and maternal. Mark and Lainey kissed me and waved goodbye as I zipped out the door.

The November air was chilly and smelled of burning leaves. On the short drive to Amy's house, I mulled over what to say when I met her and her family. I had managed not to screw things up with Nita and Tim, and, if the conversation lulled, I could certainly wax eloquent about Lainey's adoption story, which I never tired of sharing anyway.

Pulling into the driveway, I surveyed the neat neighborhood of modest cookie-cutter homes and took a deep breath as I sent an appeal heavenward. *Give me wisdom.*

A girl who was built like a small boy answered the door. Amy was petite and had no hips or curves of any kind—with one exception. She had the enviable bust line of a Barbie doll. Her brown hair was cut into a shoulder-length bob, and her almond-shaped blue eyes smiled with intelligence.

"Hi!" I exclaimed enthusiastically, the old cheerleader in me taking hold before I could wrap Amy in a hug.

Amy motioned me inside and introduced me to her mother, Penny, and her two younger siblings before we all plopped down together in the living room.

Penny broke the ice immediately by rambling on with an endorsement of her daughter's finer points.

"Everybody *loves* Amy," she crowed. "Just ask anybody. Our neighbors, my friends from work, they all go on and on about how wonderful she is."

I glanced at Amy, and she raised her eyebrows and shrugged.

Amy's mom had long brown hair with freshly-minted blond highlights and appeared to be a decade or so older than I was. Penny was pretty, youthfully dressed, and did not carry the extra pounds of many women in their forties. Her penchant for superfluous chatter, though, did nothing to enhance her beauty.

Amy stared into her lap as Penny powered on.

"Amy used to model, you know," she gushed, "and you should have seen her when she was little. Oh, she was the cutest thing!"

Amy was lovely, but I wondered why her mother was laying it on so thick.

I sensed that Amy was getting uncomfortable with her mother's over-selling, and I couldn't blame her. If anyone should be spinning a sales pitch, it was me. I was the one in the hot seat, vying to become Amy's baby-mama.

I smiled gently at Penny, saying with my eyes, *I come in peace. Chill.*

Steering the conversation in a new direction, I turned toward Amy.

"When are you due?" I asked. "And how are you feeling?"

Penny pounced.

"Oh, Amy has had such a hard time sleeping," she said. "She's had heartburn and swollen ankles. She's due January the twenty-sixth, and her next doctor's appointment is on Tuesday. We have to write a list of things to ask him!"

Penny also took the time to regale me with the details of her own pregnancy experiences and how similar these were to Amy's. Our conversation continued in this manner, with my pointedly asking Amy questions and Penny swooping in, leaving any care for her daughter's thoughts in the dust.

After about an hour of this soliloquy, Penny excused herself to tidy up in the kitchen and get her younger children ready for bed. I offered up a silent prayer of thanks that Amy and I would finally have the opportunity to catch up.

I learned that she had already connected with a counselor at another agency across town, which could make things difficult for Mark and me. Our home study would transfer anywhere, but we had a solid relationship with AA and neither the desire nor the energy to jump through another organization's hoops.

Switching agencies could lengthen the process considerably, and the baby was due in less than two months! Before I could voice my concerns, Amy piped up.

"I don't mind going through your agency."

I breathed a sigh of relief, not just because of her flexibility but because Amy had made this decision without even consulting her mother. She wanted us!

When Penny sailed back into the living room and settled into an overstuffed chair, Amy filled her in. Amy and I had made a dinner date for Chili's the following week so she could meet Mark. Penny sprang up again at the news that Amy had apparently selected her baby's adoptive parents and began painting her vision for the birth family/adoptive family relationship.

"Oh, it will be wonderful," she declared. "After the baby's born, we'll have you over for our family Christmas parties so everyone can meet you. We can even do weekend getaways at our favorite little place up north!"

I tried to hide my horror. Penny's interpretation of adoption involved a sort of joint-custody scheme. As she droned on, I heard the distinct sound of red flags flapping in the breeze.

Our openness arrangement with Nita and Tim had been so minimal and effortless—an exchange of pictures and letters until Lainey's 18th birthday—that I hadn't considered that baby number two's plan could include visitation rights.

I focused on Penny's lips as they moved, but my mind had checked out. I envisioned our Lainey at five and then 10 years old, waving goodbye to her little sister as she left for a weekend with her birth mom. Then I imagined our family of four hanging out with Amy's family while Lainey puzzled over where *her* birth parents were.

My maternal instincts fired and revved into hyperdrive. I was not willing to sacrifice my daughter's sense of wholeness on the altar of expanding the Rollandini clan. Adding another child to our ranks was not a matter of manifest destiny.

I hugged Amy goodbye that evening, telling her that we would see her in a couple of days, but, as I sped home, I realized that my bubble had burst.

Between working, keeping our marriage healthy, raising our daughter, and maintaining music and youth ministry commitments at our church, Mark and I barely had time to hang out with the friends and family we'd known forever. How would we fit a new (and volatile) set of family dynamics into our lives?

I flipped the problem over in my head like a Rubik's Cube, but I could not crank the colored squares into place. Mark and I would follow through with our dinner date with Amy, but I already knew that this adoption was never going to work.

Dinner Date

Mark and I sat across from Amy in a booth in the dimly lit restaurant, making conversation that barely scratched the surface. We had picked Amy up for our little date an hour earlier, which had allowed Penny and the kids to meet Mark briefly and—I was sure—measure him up as "father material."

The 20-minute ride to Chili's had sparked an immediate connection between Mark and Amy. As it turned out, the two of them shared the same quirky sense of humor, playing easily off one another and filling our Chevy Malibu with a comfortable camaraderie. At least for the moment, we seemed to be all in the adoption boat together.

Over dinner, Mark skillfully guided the conversation toward the matter at hand: Amy's pregnancy and her adoption plan. Without Penny there to hijack Amy's thoughts, we were able to gain a clearer picture of her desires for this baby.

Again, I could see Amy's face turn reflective as she selected which parts of her story to share and how. She looked down while she narrated, as if she were watching scenes of her life play out on her plate of chicken quesadillas. Amy had been stationed in the army in Germany and living the life one might expect of a teenager far from home.

When she was not on duty, she had found plenty of opportunities to socialize with her fellow soldiers. Finding herself pregnant with no boyfriend to speak of, her closest friends and confidants steered her toward abortion as the only real option. Of course, it was the easiest and most practical choice. Terminating the pregnancy would allow Amy to serve out her terms of enlistment and pick up afterward without a blip, but she recoiled at this part of her story.

"I never would have done that," she said, shaking her head. "I couldn't punish a baby for the choices I made. It wasn't her fault."

Amy's steely resolve stirred in me a tender respect for her. I knew women who had made a different choice.

Amy took a long, ragged breath and looked up from her plate. Her blue eyes held a question and scanned our faces for the answer. I hope she detected acceptance and admiration. The last eight years had wrought a monumental change in my perspective. It is what we hold close in the dark—an awareness of our own brokenness—that opens us to others' pain. Our wounds are access points for God's restorative labor. Clearly, Amy and I had both been surprised by our own helplessness, our need for grace.

Amy dragged a napkin across her mouth.

"I want my baby to have a mom *and* a dad. I want her to have her own room and so many other things I just can't give her right now," she explained. "You and Mark can give her all of it. I think this is what God wants me to do. Don't you?"

Before Lainey was born, when we were desperate to be called "Mom" and "Dad" by a child of our own, our answer would have been an unequivocal "yes." But with Penny's interpretation of adoption still running through my mind in Technicolor, I asked Amy about *her* hopes and dreams for this baby, *her* interpretation of openness in adoption.

To our relief, Amy's proposal for life after the baby was born—though still leaning toward more openness than with Lainey's adoption—was more palatable than Penny's chummy approach.

Amy wanted two or three face-to-face visits with us and the baby for the first few years. After that, she was amenable to whatever arrangement we deemed appropriate.

I once again flashed forward to Lainey as a preschooler, scrambling up the monkey bars or skimming down the slide at a local park while Mark and I sat in the shade of an old oak visiting with her sister's birth family. Such a young Lainey and her toddling baby sister would be oblivious to the significance of a birth-family visit. The girls would probably not even recall these meetings as the years went by, so I didn't fear this early contact somehow damaging them. At the same time, I believed that watching her baby grow up secure in our family would give Amy confidence in her adoption plan and a sense of closure.

Although Mark and I would not have initiated this sort of openness, I was reasonably certain it wouldn't jeopardize the security of our fledgling family.

On the ride home, Amy and I discussed her upcoming appointments, and she asked if I would be her driver and join her in the exam room for weekly check-ups. She had no vehicle, and both her mom and stepdad worked full-time.

"Of course," I told her, "I wouldn't want to miss a single thing!"

We dropped Amy off at home that night with a new, albeit shaky, sense that this adoption might work out. She was sincere in her plan. She also had a conviction that would enable her to follow through with the adoption. I wasn't so sure, however, how much Penny's influence would cloud Amy's vision.

As we moved through the adoption process, Penny's presence was a glaring question mark. On the one hand, she seized every opportunity to offer Amy a stream of unsolicited advice. On the other, she was curiously absent on practical matters, like taking Amy to appointments or providing maternity clothes. (Amy still wore her pre-pregnancy jeans, unbuttoned at the top.)

Would the disparity between Amy and Penny's ideas lead to a failed adoption two months down the road? This felt like a very real possibility. Mark and I were in a trust walk with God, wearing blindfolds as we crept through a relational minefield.

After our dinner date, Amy and I chatted daily. We saw each other not only for doctor's appointments but for frequent outings to dinner or the movies. Amy was sick of being cooped up at home while her family was off at work or school, so we became fast friends. She and Penny even swung by our house one day to meet Lainey and get a tour.

Mark and I had moved Lainey from the nursery into a toddler bed across the hall a week earlier, in preparation for the new baby's arrival. Penny and Amy nodded their heads, pleased at the sight of the nursery, freshly cleaned after Lainey's move, with white crib and a yellow glider for late-night feedings and lullabies. After ambling from the nursery into Lainey's room, Penny and Amy both kneeled on the floor as Lainey gave them the toddler's version of the décor; bright pink walls, an oversized flower border growing from the baseboard, and a carriage-house lantern with flickering light made Lainey's room a magical garden.

Amy was elated to have me at her weekly check-ups at the city clinic, and this time together allowed me to be a part of pregnancy in a way I hadn't yet experienced. Every weigh-in and belly measurement fascinated me, and the sound of the baby's heartbeat—a swishing kind of galloping cadence—made me catch my breath.

I sat in on a follow-up ultrasound, which the doctor had ordered in Amy's ninth month, to confirm that the measurements from the first ultrasound done at the army base in Germany were on track.

On the screen, we saw a perfectly formed head and rounded belly, skeletal fingers and toes, and confirmed that the baby was a girl—a girl who, indeed, would be arriving within the month. January 26 was her due date, precisely nine months after I had started praying for our unknown baby and birth mom.

An introvert at heart, I found that sharing my life and home in such an intimate way with near strangers—and having Amy share her life with me—was a stretch. Although I sometimes wanted to climb into bed and escape these new demands, I was also grateful that I would be able to tell our daughter this part of her story.

If this adoption worked out (and I still thought about the arrangement as one big "if"), I could, over the coming years, help our daughter understand what made her birth mother tick. But taking Amy to the doctor or even to dinner required me to find quality care for Lainey or land a substitute teacher who was proficient in sign language. I was spinning one plate too many, and it felt like they would all come clattering down at any moment.

Two weeks after Amy's ultrasound, I settled into a plastic chair in the clinic waiting room while Amy waddled off to give her routine urine specimen. As I waited, I took in the scene around me. Maple Street Clinic* was a federally-funded center that provided services for patients with limited access to health care. Its providers saw a diverse group of people with needs that included primary care, women's health, pediatrics, dental, vision, behavioral health, and mental health.

As Michigan's second largest city, GR boasted a medical mile that included an excellent children's hospital and state-of-the-art cancer and heart facilities. Meanwhile, tucked away from January wind, Grand Rapid's underclass huddled together in this clinic waiting room, joined by expectant mothers whose uneasiness seemed palpable. I watched in awe as a portly nurse gently guided a hunched woman back to the exam area. A young doctor sat knee-to-knee with a man with ragged clothes and missing teeth.

Every time Amy and I exited the clinic, I itched to lock my doors and take a nice, long bath in Purell. At the same time, I suspected that, if Jesus were strolling around this city, Maple Street Clinic is exactly the place he would stop to hang out.

When Amy finished in the bathroom, she motioned me back to a smaller waiting area before a nurse led us into the exam room. A friendly nurse in pink scrubs measured Amy and recorded her vitals. Then she sat down and gave Amy a furrowed smile.

"Everything looks great," she announced, "except—"

"Except what?" Amy interrupted.

"Well," the nurse continued, "your blood pressure is a little high, and you've got some protein in your urine, which means we need to keep an eye on you."

Keep an eye on her? I thought. *I'm going to need a little more information, Nurse Betty!*

"Um…for what?" I interjected, hoping to play the role of responsible older sister rather than control-freak adoptive mom.

"Toxemia," the nurse explained, "or preeclampsia. Same thing. Sometimes pregnancy can cause high blood pressure, which leads to all sorts of problems with the mama and the baby, but don't you worry. We're not going to let anything happen to you"—she glanced over at Amy and patted her bulging belly—"or this little girl. But we need to see you back here in a few days for a recheck to make sure everything looks OK."

We scheduled Amy's next appointment and, since I was feeling a little protective of Amy and our baby, I opted to shower her with love in one of the best ways I knew how. Time for fajitas and ice cream!

TMI

Mark put Lainey to bed that night, so the information junkie in me could learn more about toxemia/preeclampsia. Holed up in our basement office with a cup of tea at my fingertips, I googled my way through article after article about the condition, which manifests itself in severe headaches, blurred vision, shoulder or abdominal pain, nausea and vomiting, confusion or anxiety, and shortness of breath. One source tied preeclampsia to a risk of brain injury, impaired kidney and liver function, seizures, and maternal and infant death.

My eyes bugged out at this description and a memory jolted me. It was of an *ER* episode featuring a story in which an adorable couple in their 30s is expecting their first baby. When they arrive at the ER, the woman is complaining of abdominal pain and having to pee every five seconds. By the end of the episode, the mother is diagnosed with preeclampsia and ultimately dies shortly after giving birth. In the last scene, the audience watches Dr. Green through the nursery window as he enters and sits down across from the dad, rocking his newborn son, and informs the new father that he is a widower.

So, preeclampsia is pretty much like the nurse at the clinic told Amy and me, I concluded. Easy breezy, nothing to worry about. Except exactly the opposite.

Despite my new understanding of preeclampsia, when I picked up Amy for her appointment two days later, I kept the conversation light. I didn't want my fears to trigger anxiety in Amy or send her blood pressure through the roof.

Sitting side by side in the bucket seats of my Chevy Malibu, I pitched silly jokes at Amy, and she quipped back in good form. We giggled all the way to the clinic and up its steps when I suddenly realized that I would seriously miss Amy after the baby was born.

Walking through Amy's pregnancy—and the domestic drama that encircled her life—had forged a sister-like connection. With her due date two weeks away, we were both returning to daily lives that didn't revolve around one other. I would re-enter the swamp of diapers and sleepless nights, and Amy would return to a job search and college applications.

I breathed a sigh of relief when I saw that Nurse T was on duty, the same good-natured nurse who had seen Amy earlier in the week.

After Amy heaved her swollen belly onto the exam table and I settled into the plastic chair, I felt a little silly about having spent the last 48 hours catastrophizing over an *ER* episode. Amy was young, took walks, and ate her vegetables. There was no reason to think that the next two weeks wouldn't end with the routine delivery of a healthy baby and a happily recovering birth mom. With my newfound certainty, I hopped up from the chair, patted Amy on the belly, and gave her a winning smile. *Everything's going to be OK.*

First things first. Nurse T checked the baby's heartbeat (normal) then fastened a blood pressure cuff around Amy's right arm. I trained my eagle eyes on the nurse as she cocked her head, listening. Unfortunately, I'd never gotten the hang of interpreting the practiced poker faces of medical professionals.

Normally chatty and jovial, Nurse T was aloof and serious as she took Amy's pulse. Was something up or did this lady just hate Tuesdays?

"OK, Honey," she ordered, "I want you to lie down on your left side and relax for a few minutes. I think you might be a little geared up about this appointment today. I'm going to go out and check your urine, and then I'll be in to take your blood pressure and pulse again. Try to take some deep breaths, OK?"

Amy nodded compliantly as Nurse T whisked out.

"Can I get you anything, Amy?" I asked. "Are you comfortable?"

She was facing away from me with nothing to do but stare at the blank beige wall.

"No," she breathed, "but what do you think this means?"

I mentally shook a finger at my anxiety, telling it to take a hike. It was my turn to practice that poker face. I placed my hand gently on Amy's back.

"I'm sure it's fine, Amy," I lied. "You're in good hands, and you know Nurse T won't let you leave here if she has any concerns!"

Nurse T barreled in a minute later to repeat the blood pressure and pulse readings.

"Amy," she began, "the protein levels in your urine are really high, along with your blood pressure and pulse. These are all signs of preeclampsia, like we talked about at your last appointment. You need to go straight from here to the emergency room. They'll be ready for you when you get there."

Amy was still silent, so I spoke up.

"What are they going to do in the ER? Is the baby OK? Will they be able to get Amy's blood pressure under control? Is she going to be admitted?"

Nurse T gave me a weak smile.

"I really can't tell you any more than that," she said. "I'm sorry."

She squeezed Amy's hand.

"They will evaluate you at the hospital, honey, and decide on a plan from there, but you need to go right now."

Nurse T said in an urgent whisper, "Get this girl to the hospital."

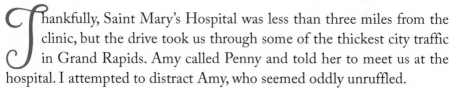

CHAPTER 16

A Little Faith

hankfully, Saint Mary's Hospital was less than three miles from the clinic, but the drive took us through some of the thickest city traffic in Grand Rapids. Amy called Penny and told her to meet us at the hospital. I attempted to distract Amy, who seemed oddly unruffled.

Even after Nurse T's gravity, Amy strolled into the ER like she was walking into Wendy's to order a Frosty.

When Amy gave her name at the front desk, the nurse checked her glowing computer screen and bounded up to ease Amy into a wheelchair. I followed behind them into a dorm room of sorts, with long rows of beds on each wall separated by wraparound curtains.

No sooner had Amy had slipped on a faded backless gown than a triage team zipped in to evaluate her and zipped out without sharing an update.

In my experience, this little scene was the epitome of emergency room care: medical staff engaged in a flurry of activity while leaving patients stranded in the dark. Sure, we figured the people in white would return to administer care, but when?

Two hours later, a nurse bustled in to report. She resembled the farmer's wife in the *American Gothic* painting.

Amy's blood pressure and pulse were elevated, she told us. Amy was leaking protein in her urine and was preeclamptic. This did not qualify as news.

But wait, there was more! I searched for the moral of the story as the nurse waxed medical. When she left, Amy and I debriefed.

"Did she say 'induce'?" we both asked.

Penny rushed in around 7:00 p.m., breathless and looking like she'd just downed a double shot of espresso with a Red Bull chaser. Before Amy and I could fill her in, a young doctor swung in.

"This pregnancy is making Amy sick," he said, flipping through the stack of notes on his clipboard, "and the only way to make her better is for her to deliver the baby. As soon as a room is open, we'll get her settled and begin induction."

His head jerked up as though he suddenly remembered he was addressing actual people. "Any questions?"

Yes, in fact, Penny had a list.

As she grilled the doctor, who looked like a deer caught in headlights, I stepped outside the curtain to call Mark. He picked up on the first ring, and I told him what I knew.

"Does this mean…" His voice trailed off. I couldn't quite wrap my brain around it either. Mark and I both thought we had at least two more weeks. I was thrilled but a little daunted.

"Yep," I confirmed, "the baby's coming." I heard Lainey babbling away on the other end of the line. Our two-year-old would have to hold on tight over the next couple of days as we brought in a bevy of neighbors to babysit while we focused on her sister.

Mark's rich baritone broke into my pondering. "I'm on my way."

When I stepped back through the curtain, the doctor had disappeared, and Penny and Amy were engrossed in a conversation about baby names.

"Definitely Mackenzie," Amy announced firmly.

This conversation about naming the baby—the one that was supposed to belong to Mark and me—didn't throw me too much. While the birth mother's name for the baby always went on the hospital birth certificate, another birth certificate was issued later with the name given by the adoptive parents. Amy had shared her baby name list at our first meeting while we listened politely and offered our most filtered of thoughts.

I myself had started making a mental list of baby names in ninth grade, at roughly the moment I'd begun doodling the last name of my latest crush on my spiral bound notebooks. Of course, the list evolved. I crossed off "Alicia," a name I once considered feminine and flowing, when it became too popular. I gave "Shay" the axe when I dated a farm boy named Shay who emanated *eau de cattle*. "Mackenzie" had never made the list, for good reason. Mark and I had known a string of girls named Mackenzie, all bold and brash and without a lick of humility.

Throwing caution to the wind, I revealed the name that Mark and I had chosen. The name hadn't been on any list but had occurred to me with a conviction equal to its meaning.

"Faith," I said reverently. The word came out like a prayer. "Mark and I were thinking 'Faith.'"

Penny warmed to the name immediately but not in the way I intended. "Oh, 'Mackenzie Faith'...I love it!" she declared. "It's perfect!"

Penny had an amazing capacity to misunderstand me, her daughter, and adoption etiquette. To be fair, though, I was a bit bold to broach this topic when we were within hours of bringing the baby home—and my courage ended there. I left Penny in her oblivion and took comfort in knowing Amy and I were on the same page.

In the last two months, I had called the agency multiple times—panicky and perplexed—to talk with Shelley about Penny's ideas. Ideas like attending the baby's birthday parties and regular babysitting and play dates with "Grandma." I could always count on Shelley to gently talk me off the ledge.

"Your agreement is not with Penny, it's with Amy," she reminded me. "What does Amy say about openness?"

I chanted Shelley's words to myself as I bit my tongue in half and prayed for Penny to do the same.

Game Plan

Finally, the orderlies moved Amy to a birthing room. Dull wallpaper made the room strangely cozy, but there was a lot more medical equipment than I remembered from Lainey's birth. The doctor on call joined us shortly. She stood beside Amy's bed to rattle off the birthing plan.

Penny broke in to cross-examine the doctor.

"What is this drug you're using to induce?" Penny demanded.

The doctor opened her mouth to answer, but Penny held up a finger and shoved it toward the small woman. With the other hand, she plucked up the room phone and punched in a number.

Amy and I stared. It was like watching the *Jerry Springer Show*.

"I'm going to call my friend about this. She's a midwife."

Dr. Jansen blinked a few times, squared her shoulders and continued, this time addressing Amy directly. I listened carefully as she explained the protocol.

Meanwhile, Penny chatted with her midwife friend and updated the doctor with her insight.

I watched Amy's head bob from side to side, trying to give Dr. Jansen and her mom equal time. I didn't dare tell Penny to shut up, though the impulse burned so hot within me I was sure flames would shoot out of my mouth if I opened it.

I pictured myself in a silent black-and-white film, smacking Penny across the face and shaking her by the shoulders with the subtitle, *Get a hold of yourself, woman!*

Couldn't Penny see that she was adding to her daughter's stress?

Dr. Jansen wrapped up her instructions just as Penny hung up the receiver.

"We are not going to use that drug that you mentioned," Penny announced. "It causes uterine rupture in 0.02% of inductions."

A fog of silent tension filled the room.

My inner snark begged for release, but, whatever I might have said, there was no doubt I would later regret it. I considered retorts like, "Where exactly did your friend go to med school?" and, "If Amy had wanted a midwife, she would have chosen a midwife, you psycho." Mature responses like that.

The doctor sized up Penny and also appeared to be measuring her words before letting them pour forth. Wise move.

"Fine," Doctor Jansen said, "we'll use a different medication," and then she marched from the room, white coat sailing behind her.

I could only imagine the conversations that would take place in the hospital's on-call room that night. And this baby had only begun to make her way here.

Slow Progress

Once we'd finally arrived at a plan for Amy's preeclampsia, a stream of medical professionals tramped in and out of the room in their soft-soled orthopedic shoes.

The plan was this: Before beginning induction, they would start Amy on a loading dose of magnesium sulfate, which would continue until the baby arrived. Magnesium sulfate—or "mag," as the staff called it—would reduce Amy's chance of seizures. In the meantime, the nurses would monitor her blood pressure and the baby's heart rate.

When Amy was settled comfortably in bed, surrounded by a labyrinth of tubes and wires, she asked me to bring Mark in from the hallway. I was glad to have a buffer between me and Penny but a bit concerned that Mark and Penny would go *tête-à-tête*. Mark usually offered his thoughts without filter, and stifling them in such close quarters would take an act of God.

We visited amiably for an hour, hovering on safe subjects like food and the weather, before another doctor swept in at shift change to tell Amy the induction would take a while. Possibly a long while.

Amy had technically been in labor for a couple hours, but she couldn't feel a thing, except a hardening of her belly, visible as a hilly peak on the monitor's steady readout. At this pace, Amy would be able to get a good night's sleep. Mark was next to me looking wiped, and I was jonesing for some shuteye.

I glanced over at the stiff, pink chair in the birthing room and imagined the tossing and turning involved in trying to rest there with the napkin of a blanket we might be able to score from a nurse. Just thinking about it made me tired and cold. Before Lainey, I never would've considered leaving the birth mom at the hospital—but motherhood had removed my blinders.

We had a toddler at home who had a cool new bed without bars and no qualms about rising every hour to wake Mommy and Daddy. Realistically, I needed to bank some sleep to be able to support Amy through the next 24 hours of labor and to have the energy needed to cuddle, change, and feed the newest Rollandini. So, with Penny and Amy's promise to call us with any update, Mark and I slogged home.

Delivery & Doubting

I was able to catch a few Z's before returning to the hospital at 7:30 the next morning.

Amy was smiling when I strolled in to see a sleepy Penny resting in the pink chair. Not much had changed in eight hours, except that Amy was starting to feel those pesky contractions.

"I feel like I have my own personal furnace heating me from the inside out," she complained.

Amy's rise in body temperature and flushed face were innocuous side effects of the magnesium sulfate.

I asked her if I could get her anything, but it was a silly question. Although she was ravenous, she wasn't allowed to eat and didn't feel like reading. What saint, after all, would fancy a good book while trying to pass what is basically a seven-pound kidney stone?

As an alternative to *Beowulf*, we switched on the TV to a succession of vapid morning talk shows.

By 11:00 a.m., Amy's labor had begun in earnest. Contractions had her twisting with discomfort in her small bed.

I summoned Mark to the hospital, and when he arrived an hour later, hard labor had descended on our friend. We wanted to spare the 19-year-old the experience of having a grown man in the room while she contorted in a backless gown. Our hospital plan had been different with Nita, who already had a daughter and a decade more life experience.

Penny and I flanked Amy, holding her hands through each contraction, dabbing her forehead with a cool washcloth, and taking turns running to the bathroom to freshen the cloth. For the first time, Penny and I were on the same team, and I felt a sudden burst of affection for the woman. She could have easily shut me out of the birth process but had taken the opposite route.

Just then, God nudged me toward compassion. Penny was struggling to hold the pieces of her family together, just as I was fighting for mine. Our respective resilience united us, and it struck me that Penny's need for control might flow from her lifetime experience of powerlessness. I would be a fool not to realize how much society could marginalize a working-class, functionally single mother of four.

Besides, Penny was on the brink of meeting her very first grandchild only to say goodbye to her. This, I concluded, entitled her to a little bit of crazy and propelled me toward a little bit of grace.

Around 3:00 p.m., the nurses directed Amy to push.

At 3:30, she was exhausted and angry.

"I can't do this anymore," she cried. "Just get her out!"

But the nurses chanted, "Just one more push, just one more push. You're doing great, honey!"

Clearly the medical definition of "one more" wasn't based in mathematical reality. Each time Amy made it through one push, she could barely catch her breath before the chorus of, "Just one more push, one more push!" resumed.

The nurses were compelling actors, but Amy was on to their game. Her face was blotchy, and sweat had plastered her hair to her temples in spirals.

"I'm too tired," Amy pleaded, "I just can't do this. It's too hard. Is it normal for labor to take this long?"

The nurses looked at each other, amused, and the ring leader took over.

"This is totally normal, Amy," she reassured, "and you're doing so great! You're almost there! You can do this!"

As Amy worked through another push, the baby's head—covered in dark, wet whorls of hair—was crowning.

It was the fourth time I had been a witness to the "miracle of life", but I was freshly in awe. A new soul was about to make her appearance and I would be a witness.

Amy pushed once more and the baby's head squeezed out, followed by shoulders and the rest of her slick frame. Before the nurse even snipped the umbilical cord, I noted her perfectly formed arms and legs, 10 wrinkled fingers and 10 toes. I also observed her skin tone—warm ebony—with a removed sort of surprise. *Our baby is African American!* I thought. *Well, that's something we didn't consider.*

I could not have been more surprised if a baby boy had bounced out of Amy's womb and started reciting the Declaration of Independence. My surprise didn't reflect disappointment—it reflected the fact that the adoption paperwork I had signed in blood was, apparently, inaccurate.

The birth mom always discloses the baby's ethnicity and identifies the biological father somewhere in the adoption process, and Amy had told us unequivocally that this baby was white.

I jotted notes on my mental to-do list:

1. *Attend African-American hair-care classes.*
2. *Move to a more heterogeneous community.*

Our Midwest town was predominantly populated with white faces, albeit friendly, but that would never do for raising a happy mixed-race daughter with a healthy sense of identity.

Right about the time I had identified more inclusive neighborhoods for our move, the baby's complexion began to lighten. I later learned that her darkened skin was a temporary side effect of the magnesium sulfate. Either way, this kiddo was ours. At least, I hoped.

I hugged Amy. "You're a trooper, girl!" I exclaimed. "She's beautiful!"

Twenty-four hours of labor had exhausted the teenager. Amy held the baby for a few minutes and then closed her eyes as Penny reached down to take the child.

I zipped into the hallway to grab Mark, who hadn't received an update since the pushing began, and was relieved when Penny generously handed the swaddled bundle to me.

She leaned over my shoulder so we could admire in unison. Even after Penny had begun bonding with the baby, she seemed to acknowledge that Mark and I were a part of the deal. Though the adoption was far from finished, I interpreted this as a positive omen.

After the nurses gently shooed our little party into the hallway so Amy could rest, we lingered outside the room for a while, passing the tiny elf around under the harsh fluorescent lighting. Like Amy, everything about this baby was miniature, except for a huge goose egg on the top of her head—a souvenir from her jaunt down the birth canal. Her heart-shaped lips and Bambi eyelashes made me ponder if she'd been delivered by fairies.

A few minutes later, the nurses broke up our fan club and whisked the baby to the nursery for more neonatal protocol. Exhausted from her night in the pink chair, Penny gave us quick hugs and sped home.

Mark and I mapped out the next 12 hours. He would go home and share the news with Lainey and our parents and I would stay put. We brushed lips before he left, and I then scuttled down to the nursery for some alone time with Mackenzie/Faith.

I crept into the small corner room like a kid on Christmas morning. When I opened the door, the smell of fresh linen and astringent filled my nostrils. The space held about 10 bassinets but only three had babies. I reached over the side of the bassinet and scooped ours into my arms. She was sleeping soundly, and I walked over to a wooden rocker to get properly acquainted. I wanted my connection with her—whether fleeting or permanent—to begin post haste.

I wished for the sky to part and bathe the nursery in rays of heavenly light as I sat for the first time with Faith. I longed for a sign from God that this baby was ours. Holding Faith made me vulnerable, and I felt the uncertainty of our situation. Even if Amy could sustain the courage to cement the adoption, I didn't see how Penny could or would. I'd spent the last several hours watching a grandmother gaze at her granddaughter, and I recognized the heavy task of Penny's letting her go.

I stared intently at this baby—my Faith—as I rocked back and forth in the quiet nursery. Despite hospital staff trooping past the large windows, I felt very much alone. I wanted to pray but was helpless to string together words to communicate my longing for closure, my need for assurance about God's good plans for our small family and for Faith. So, I sang the most dependable words in reach.

Amazing grace how sweet the sound that saved a wretch like me. I once was lost, but now I'm found, was blind but now I see.

Faith stirred in her sleep and let out a squeaky yawn before settling again.

'Twas grace that taught my heart to fear and grace my fears relieved. How precious did that grace appear the hour I first believed.

I closed my eyes and bent to kiss Faith on her downy head, breathing in the smell of newborn. Could I commit this memory—of the heft of her body, the smoothness of her cheek—to a place inside of me where it could never be taken away? I strung together a chain of lullabies, and the minutes ticked by until my songs ran out. I studied Faith's face with a peaceful sort of empty and looked for a sign; there was no hint of anything, save Faith's unworried slumber.

I didn't know if this was the beginning of our life together or the end of it, but one seemed just as likely as the other. In these wee hours, at least, I *was* this little one's mama, and I would do my part. I could offer warmth and a safe place to rest. When she cried, I could speak comfort. This night might be all we had, but, for now, I would welcome it with joy.

CHAPTER 17

Confusion & Comfort

I awoke the next morning in Amy's new room on the firm fold-down next to her bed; sometime after 2:00 a.m., sleep deprivation had driven me from the nursery in search of rest. After showering in the small private bathroom, I ambled out to find Amy sitting up and enjoying a breakfast of pancakes and eggs, applesauce and chocolate milk. She was off the magnesium, so her normal ivory complexion had replaced the blotchy crimson. I wondered if our relationship would be awkward now that labor and delivery were over, but we instantly fell into our groove.

When the nurses wheeled the baby's bassinet into the room, I changed her diaper and placed her in Amy's arms. She cuddled Faith while I tidied up and then handed the newborn back to me. Amy and I focused on the baby and began to contemplate the changes ahead. Because of Amy's pre-eclampsia, the nurses monitored her closely and ordered one more night in the hospital until the magnesium had fully left her system.

Penny whisked in later that morning, followed by Mark's brief visit.

A steady stream of Amy's friends and family filed in and out into the afternoon. A few aunts and cousins visited, including one aunt who worked as a nurse on the hospital's cardiac floor. Some of Amy's people offered me warm smiles; others treated me like a ghost.

It was hard to discern my role during these visits. Should I give Amy and her visitors privacy? Did they want to meet the adoptive mom or ask me questions? It was an awkward dance to find a balance between being present enough to prove that I cared and absent enough to avoid becoming a nuisance.

One particular aunt, a woman in her forties with hair stuck in the '80s, turned her back to me and spoke to Amy in hushed tones. With Amy, I knew where I stood, but with these relatives, I often felt like the villain. I was the woman who had come to snatch poor Amy's baby.

When Amy's guests invited me into their conversation, I endeavored to convey my gratitude for Amy's selflessness. I hoped to win the "Best Adoptive Mom Pageant" and to hear Amy's family walk away saying, "Oh, that Sarah is such a nice lady, what a lucky baby!"

As it turned out, my overworked kindness was exhausting, and I resented having to put on a show.

This is something people don't tell you about adoption, how—if you've already experienced infertility—the adoption process might again ram you up against the wall of your old friends: powerlessness and anger. You thought you'd said good riddance to the duo long ago—perhaps when you got the phone call or met that birth mom who chose you.

But as I stood like a spectator in Amy's bright hospital room and watched strangers play hot potato with my baby, my sense of injustice bubbled up.

Infertility was a thief that had ransacked my naïveté, my sense of control over my own body and even my own babies; now the opportunity to celebrate my child's birth free from thoughts of *What if I lose her?* had also evaporated. I hungered for my own tribe to be there holding our daughter, admiring her long lashes and her thatch of dark hair.

Yes, Amy was giving up her baby, and, yes, this hospital time belonged to her. But I was no Mother Teresa and so couldn't deny my own losses in the adoption process.

Besides, repressing my pain had never actually sent it packing. My sorrow had instead morphed into entitlement. So, as I slouched in the shadows of the dim hospital room, I acknowledged that grain of sand between the sheets, my ugly self-pity. Only the luxurious comfort of my God allowed me to brush it away and recall that he'd never promised me a life without trouble, only that his kindness would offset his sometimes difficult plans for Team Rollandini.

Rocky Relations

That evening, after all the visitors had dispersed and it was just Penny, Amy, and me, I sat in another upright pink chair feeding the baby. Her mouth fascinated me as it puckered and un-puckered while her chin bobbed up and down with each swallow. Missing the rocker from the nursery, I swayed gently from side to side as Faith's eyelids fluttered sleepily.

"What are you doing?" Penny's voice rang with annoyance. She was talking to me.

"What do you mean?" I asked sincerely, bracing myself.

"You're rocking back and forth while she's eating," Penny spat, as though baby manuals had banned the practice without exception. "You're making me sick just watching you."

"Oh," I responded then pursed my lips to hold back the nasty words I could already taste.

If feeding and rocking a baby was a no-no, I would have to deprogram every sister-in-law, aunt, cousin, and grandmother in my family. Babies and rocking went together like warm chocolate-chip cookies and cold milk. Also, I was already a mother to a girl whom rocking had served quite well, thank you very much.

But given Penny's obvious aversion to the practice, I swallowed my pride—and what little sense of control I still possessed—and eased my body to a halt.

After Amy settled down for the night and the nurse wheeled the baby to the nursery, I excused myself to make some phone calls. I planned to stay the night again to keep Amy company and to do some more bonding with the baby.

Shuffling back toward the room, I saw Penny step out with coat on and purse slung over her shoulder. I involuntarily sighed with relief.

Spying me, though, Penny's face brightened, and she endeavored to strike up a chummy conversation in the darkened hallway.

Was she trying to make amends for her earlier slam? I could never tell from one moment to the next if Penny had made her peace with me or was scouting out any opportunity to ditch the adoptive mom.

I leaned against the wall, staring blankly at her. I had slept only a handful of the last 48 hours, and my brain was shutting down. Thankfully, the protruding wall guard that ran the length of the hallway dug into the small of my back and kept me off balance and awake. I listened half-heartedly to Penny's patter, nodding my head where appropriate and willing my eyelids to stay open. After half an hour, I slid down the wall onto the floor, folded my arms over my knees and rested my head.

Across from me, Penny followed suit, turning the page on a new chapter of discourse, this time about her volatile relationship with Amy's father. At 3:00 a.m., with the halls empty and still, Penny finally said farewell, and I collapsed on my slab next to Amy's bed.

Going Home

When pinkish light seeped in through the blinds, a peppy nurse—too much of a morning person for my taste—danced in to tell us that the doctor would sign Amy's discharge papers by noon.

After the nurse unhooked her from all of the wires, I helped Amy into the bathroom to take the shower she'd been begging for. She still moved sluggishly, so after she dressed, I offered to help blow-dry and style her hair. I took my time with her thick brown locks, thankful to serve in this small way.

While Amy finished up in the bathroom, Mark arrived with Lainey in tow, and the two of us awkwardly introduced her to her new sister. Mark held Lainey in his arms, and she pointed at the squirming parcel I cradled then wriggled away and made a beeline for the buttons on the IV equipment. Their relationship, like any, would take time.

As with Lainey's adoption, we would take Faith home that day but only on "temporary placement" until Amy signed termination papers in court.

The wait for discharge seemed interminable. Penny showed up mid-morning, and we struggled to make conversation. The awareness of the next step hung like a black cloud. After Amy's gallant efforts, she was departing empty-handed, and we were going home with her baby.

When noon came and went, I made my own beeline to the nurses' station.

144

"Um…when will the doctor be in?" I asked nonchalantly.

"Oh, he should be in soon!" she crooned.

Her glut of information was ever so helpful.

Finally, at 1:00, the doctor dashed in, checked Amy's paperwork, and scribbled out a signature. Amy was good to go, and we had used up our words in the five-hour wait. "Thank you," "We love you," and "We'll be in touch," had begun to feel glib in context.

We did, however, pause for a picture, which would help bridge the gap left by our ineloquence. In the photo, Amy and I hold the weight of Faith's small body between us while Mark peeks over my shoulder at our new daughter.

Hung on the middle of the wall behind us is a small cross, a simple pine carving with dark oak inlay. None of us was aware of the symbol's prominence when we posed that day for the picture, but I am overcome now with its weight. It signifies how God knew all along that humans would make a mess of the world and that he would reach out to rescue us. Even most agnostics and atheists are aware of the Christian belief in Jesus' death on a cross and resurrection three days later. Still, like many Christians, they fail to recognize its power.

Yes, Jesus' rising ensures a place for us in heaven. But so much more than that, his saving has the power to reclaim our pain—our mistakes—and wipe out sin's ability to destroy us. No matter how many times we miss the mark, placing our faith in Christ continues to return us to true center.

When I am bombarded by voices touting various paths to self-actualization, I press in to the burden and beauty of the cross.

Party of Four

The next two weeks were a blur of sleepless activity—feeding and diapering and dabbing at spit up—of groggy hours spent rocking Faith to sleep and whispering across the hall to Lainey that she absolutely does not need another drink of water at 3:00 a.m. With her baby sister wailing in the wee hours, she was wired for a rager most every night.

To curtail Lainey's nocturnal wandering Mark erected a plastic baby gate at the doorway to her room, which we closed at bedtime. When Lainey woke to find herself corralled, she shook the gate back and forth with her chubby toddler hands. On the off-chance I had somehow managed to lull Faith to sleep, Lainey's midnight racket startled her awake and gave us two boisterous children by night and a pair of tantrum-throwing messes by day.

Along with the adjustment of having multiple children, it felt like I was herding cats to maintain a healthy relationship with Amy (and Penny). We talked on the phone nearly every day, and, during one such conversation, as I jiggled Faith in her baby sling and swiped a crayon from Lainey's fist before she created a canvas out of our living room wall, I realized these frequent chats needed to taper off. The stresses of relational overload had shaved eight pounds off my frame.

When Faith was a couple of weeks old, I broached "the name" subject with Amy.

"We didn't get a chance to talk about this at the hospital," I hedged, "but I just wanted to let you know that we've named her 'Faith Mackenzie,' not 'Mackenzie Faith'."

I balanced the phone between my shoulder and chin, wiping chocolate from Lainey's fingers and face with a wet paper towel. She needed a bath. I needed a bath.

Amy's quiet, low voice broke in.

"I'm not sure how I feel about that," she confessed.

I steeled myself for the difficult words I must say. Amy had not been to court yet, but I refused to keep secrets out of fear she would change her mind. I was not some used car salesman cutting a quick deal. Amy deserved complete honesty, and I could live with nothing less.

"Well, Amy," I said, "I get where you're coming from, but you need to understand that if Mark and I are going to be her parents, we want to give her the name that we've chosen, that means something special to *us*."

I don't know how those words got past the knot in my chest that screamed, "Just agree with the birth mom or you'll lose your baby," but God had made me bold and obedient to his standard: Nothing but truth.

As the weeks went by, Amy's court date loomed, and our phone calls became less frequent. The strain of our constant connection evolved into a dread of the unknown. What was on Amy's mind when we weren't talking every day?

One gray February afternoon, I laid the girls down for an afternoon nap and seized the rare peaceful moment to check in with Amy. She answered after a few rings and sounded upbeat and out of breath.

"How are you doing?" I asked.

"Fine!" she replied enthusiastically. "How about you?"

Perhaps a redirect was in order.

"No, Amy," I drawled, "how *are* you? Are you feeling OK about everything?"

"Oh!" Amy exclaimed, laughing. "You mean how am I *doing!*"

"Yes," I prodded, "I'm sure Faith has been on your mind a lot with the court date coming up."

I had flung my mom apron aside to become a counselor for the moment. This new Amy seemed lighter and younger than the Amy I'd come to know over the past three months. She sounded like a giddy schoolgirl.

"Well, this is probably going to sound awful, but…" Amy trailed off. "I really haven't been thinking about her very much."

Hearing this, I breathed deeply for the first time since we brought Faith home. Many might have viewed Amy's comment as callous—how could a mother give up her child so easily?—but I saw the rightness behind her remark. These were the words of a girl who had shouldered a heavy load for 10 months, made a complex, grown-up decision and started to imagine her own future again.

It was the exhilarating freedom that most 20-year-olds jumped into without a backward glance. Amy had given her daughter a mom, a dad, and a big sister—and, in doing so, had reclaimed the life she'd taken for granted only a year earlier.

She spoke of starting college, hanging out with old friends, and attending a Kenny Chesney concert the following week.

"I finally get to see my boyfriend perform live!" she joked.

She was moving on and, though there would be scars, time would soothe the grief of letting go.

As I said goodbye and promised to reconnect with Amy soon, I knew that our paths were diverging. The realization made me feel like sprinting gleefully around the block shouting, "Freedom!" It also made me want to bury my face in a pint of chocolate chip ice cream.

Real Mom

Amy appeared in court on February 21 to terminate her parental rights. In March and April, I took the girls to the mall for a couple of visits with Amy and her family. As I watched Lainey zooming around the tree house play structure, Penny and Amy passed Faith back and forth and asked me about her feeding schedule and growth milestones. Faith had started to smile and coo in response to familiar faces. She was quite the charmer.

Amy and I penciled in a few meetings in the months leading up to Faith's first birthday, but we scrapped those plans when Amy became busy with college classes and activities.

Many friends questioned how I could tolerate sharing my daughter at these birth family outings.

"Isn't it awkward to see Faith with her 'real mom'?" they asked. "I could never handle that!"

Ugh. My friends were not yet savvy with the lingo, which seeks to honor everyone involved in the adoption process. Using the terms "biological mom" or "birth mother" strikes the right tone as does "adoptive mom", if clarification is needed. It's also appropriate for adoptive parents to say, "We have two daughters through adoption," which puts the child before the label, rather than, "We have two adopted daughters." The latter turn of phrase overemphasizes how a child is born into a family, which is as odd as stating, "We have one C-section daughter and a vaginal-birth son." Ew.

Changing the way we talk about adoption can feel like navigating through an obstacle course flowing with hot lava. And does it even matter? In short, yes. Language influences thought, which influences language. People who take the time to learn positive adoption language validate and celebrate our families. After all, if Amy was Faith's "real mom" what did that make me? Fortunately, I was caught up in being a real mom, and my friends' words no longer stung. Still, I took time to educate my tribe on appropriate terminology as part of filling them in on our visits with Amy.

In my head, I knew that Amy had carried and given birth to Faith. I had witnessed her preeclampsia and subsequent delivery of our healthy baby girl. During our visits, Amy demonstrated her natural nurturer abilities. She knew how to cuddle Faith and how to bounce her when she fussed. But watching Amy with Faith was like watching a babysitter, not some chick vying for my position as Faith's mom. This was, in part, because of Amy's empathy but also because I had engaged in the significant task of mothering. The bond between me and both of my daughters was steadfast.

Five weeks after bringing Faith home, we ate chili and watched Michigan State basketball at my parents' house. The guys chastised the refs from the front room while Mom stood in the kitchen holding Faith and stirring our dinner. Lainey and I played tickle monster in the living room as the pungent aroma of roasted tomatoes and chili pepper filled the house.

"I'm gonna get you!" I trilled, wiggling my fingers toward Lainey as she darted away, squealing in delight.

My mom broke in from the kitchen island. "Faith knows your voice," she announced. "Look! She's looking for her mama!"

I glanced over to see Faith's head swivel from side to side, searching for me. When her vision steadied on my face, the corners of her mouth wobbled up and met her eyes; it was her first true smile.

Faith's recognition of me as her mama, her caregiver, brought to mind thoughts of my own good shepherd. In John 10:27, Jesus tells his disciples, "My sheep listen to my voice; I know them and they follow me." Sheep follow the shepherd's call to wolf-free pastures of sweet clover. I followed Christ each day, knowing that doing so would not only secure heaven but a daily hope that sustained me. At two and two months, my daughters depended on me for Cheerios and chocolate milk, warm formula, clean dry bottoms and story time snuggles. If I proved myself dependable as their mommy, I could ultimately teach them to rely on the good shepherd, the one who—unlike me—would never let them down.

My girls had been birthed by two women to whom I could speak only love and gratitude. Yet through God's confounding grace, Lainey and Faith would hear *my* voice each day. They would listen and follow. I would know my children and be deeply known by them, today and in the days that God had laid ahead of us.

Tangled Trust

Two months after we brought Faith home, I crept up to Lainey's bedroom door during naptime. As I pressed my ear against the oak, I heard Lainey making animated conversation with someone. This was commonplace for our introvert who, at only two and a half, enjoyed nothing more than hours alone in her room to pretend. I cracked open the door to find her sitting up in bed. She grinned sheepishly.

"You're supposed to be sleeping, honey. Who were you talking to?" I asked.

"I was talking to God," Lainey reported.

"And what were you talking to him about?"

"I was telling him about Big Bird and Cookie Monster and Elmo."

"Uh-huh," I mumbled as my mind shifted to my long to-do list.

"He tells me the truth!" Lainey added.

I nodded, but Lainey could see that my head was elsewhere.

"Listen, Mama," she appealed, squirming to the edge of the bed until our faces were within inches, "God *always* tells the truth!"

Plenty of skeptics would chalk up our post-naptime communiqué to a Sunday school lesson Lainey was parroting, but my toddler was delivering a simple message straight from the heart of God. They were words I had claimed as my own only after our period of waiting had called God's trustworthiness into question. This was the reminder I still needed like an hourly notification on my cell phone: *Lay your burdens down. Cast all your cares upon me. My yoke is easy and my burden is light. Trust me.*

It seemed, with our family of four, Mark and I had survived the darkness of infertility, yet God had not imparted to me that our family was complete. As I slapped together Lainey's peanut butter sandwiches and spooned Faithy's sweet potatoes, I was tuned in to hear God's next direction. Was it my ingratitude shouting, "More, more, more!" or my heavenly father's abundant heart? At 35, I had learned to trust the Lord afresh, but my will and his were a basket full of knotted yarn I had rarely managed to untangle.

CHAPTER 18

The Surrogate Gestational Carrier

hen I found myself clawing at the walls of infertility's pit of despair, there were a handful of women prepared to take extreme measures right along with me. My cousin Gina. Mark's youngest sister, Joyce. Char, an acquaintance from my parents' church who had heard of our woes through the prayer chain. Even my mother, who was technically premenopausal. All of these champions had thrown their hats into the ring to be considered for the job of incubating our baby.

The depth of their compassion shocked me, but I had zero qualms about moving forward with such a plan if presented with the right fit. After all, surrogacy was number seven on the "how to have a baby" blueprint that I had scrawled out eight years earlier. It came in ahead of adoption, which was number eight. Yet none of these relationships—cousin, sister-in-law, mom, acquaintance—seemed to fit the task at hand. Every one of these plucky women was either too familiar or too far away. The thought of my mom carrying our baby, and suffering the heartburn and hemorrhoids that went along with the gig, was just plain weird. So, Mark and I had shoved surrogacy to the back burner while God led us to the slightly less sticky option of adopting.

Then there was Johnna. In January 2004, about the time Mark and I were rounding up our paperwork for adoption number two, Johnna, a friend with whom I sang in our church's worship band, broached the subject of surrogacy. As members of the servant evangelism team, Johnna and I had walked side by side in poor neighborhoods to hand out light bulbs and hold impromptu prayer circles. We had squeegeed filthy car windshields in store parking lots in the dead of winter. In these two-hour outreach blitzes, we showed up, served, and dashed back to our busy lives. Yes. Johnna and I were sisters in Christ, but we were hardly close.

That fall, after band practice in our storefront church space, Johnna approached me to ask how adoption number two was going. With long brown hair and a dimpled smile, Johnna was warm and easy-going.

"We're hoping to have a baby by this time next year," I said, giving her the *Reader's Digest* version. Not many people were truly interested in a play by play.

"That's great!" she said lightly then announced, "I wanted to tell you that I've always wanted to carry a baby for somebody." Before I could respond, Johnna rushed on. "I just never knew who I would do it for, but I think God is telling me it's supposed to be you."

I raised my eyebrows, struggling to formulate my thoughts into something coherent. Johnna took this as a sign to carry on with her mission.

"I loved being pregnant," she continued, "and we already have Zach and Cassidy. Steve and I don't want any more kids, so I would love to do this for you and Mark if you want me to."

Johnna searched my face for some reaction to her generous offer.

"No pressure!" She laughed, easing the awkwardness, and I followed suit.

"Thank you," I said, truly meaning it. "Thank you so much for the offer!"

I considered again the women who had made similar proposals before Mark and I made our decision to adopt.

"I'll think about it…and I'll talk to Mark about it," I told her. "We're in the middle of the adoption process right now, but maybe somewhere down the road. Who knows?"

"Of course!" Johnna replied enthusiastically. "No rush, I just wanted to put it out there."

It was out there. And, in truth, I wasn't so taken aback—mainly because I didn't think Johnna would follow through or that Mark and I would take her up on the offer to rent her womb.

Most "offers" for help of any kind are just that: People making attempts to appear helpful without actually rendering anything bankable. I've been guilty of this pseudo-compassion myself.

"Let me know if I can help in any way!" I've said to friends, secretly hoping they wouldn't call me to account. It wasn't that I lacked the desire to serve but rather the bandwidth.

A friend with cancer went without my handcrafted casserole so I could check off my long to-do list. My neighbor with a prodigal son would have to wait for that hot cup of tea on my couch. Sadly, the stinking pile of laundry on our mudroom floor took priority.

I suspected Johnna was a lot like me, throwing out benevolent but ultimately hollow offers. She certainly had no idea what being a "surrogate" entailed. I briefed Mark on my conversation with Johnna when I arrived home that night, and we shared a cynical laugh before filing the idea under "when pigs fly."

Two years later, Mark and I were in the throes of parenthood with a bubbly three-year-old and a one-year-old with a serious Napoleon complex. I believed that our difficulty having kids the old-fashioned way meant that it was time to consider whether or not our family was finally complete.

Mark, on the other hand, was certain that the expansion phase was over. When I raised the subject of adding another child to our brood, his refrain was, *"Aren't we enough?"*

His question echoed with the memory of past hurts. Did we really have to fling ourselves into that hot mess again, when pursuing a child had sucked the life out of our marriage and put us at the mercy of infertility treatments and vacillating birth mothers?

But my question to Mark and to God was always, "Why not one more?"

I had fond teenage memories of hanging out at my friend Renee's house, where a family of nine thrived under one roof. I considered it a challenge to keep a mental count of each Esper kid's name in birth order. If I forgot one of them, I searched for it like a Sudoku solution. Having grown up with a single sibling, I loved the hustle and bustle at Renee's house, the mini dramas unfolding in every room.

I was eager to up our game to "party of five," but Mark would need some convincing per usual. I loved that my life was now filled with library visits, floor play, and two girls who thrilled at every pebble and dandelion. Through their eyes, the mundane became a cause for worship.

Mark made other calculations. He understood that another child meant another drain on our limited resources, both emotional and financial.

He also dared to ask the more central question: How, pray tell, would we acquire a third child? Mark was 100% on board with having another baby as long as said infant dropped into our laps like manna from heaven. He was not so thrilled about jumping through more medical or legal hoops.

We had gone back and forth about pursuing baby number three for a month when we finally hauled ourselves to the front porch to settle the issue. The girls were in the middle of a nap, so we managed to keep them out of the brouhaha, though our neighbors witnessed some hand-flapping and raised voices spilling onto Sycamore Drive.

"I don't want to look back in five years and regret that we didn't have another baby!" I pleaded.

"We're just getting a handle on our home equity line," Mark reasoned. "You want to borrow money again for a third child? We're going to be right back where we started. Can't you just be happy with what we have?"

Our anger had peaked and we were gridlocked as we sat in wicker chairs for several silent minutes. I was ever angling for more, and Mark always declared, "Enough!"

I was helpless to make him see that my insistence didn't come from ingratitude but from a compulsion to share our bounty with another child. God had lavished his love on us in the gift of our daughters and parenting was a direct outpouring of that same abundance. Quite simply, I had more to give.

I delighted in my Heavenly Father's affection and even his playfulness, which anointed our days. I sensed his nearness when strangers in the grocery store stopped me to comment, "Your girls look so much like you!" and in the fierce bond between Lainey and Faith, marked by equal parts sibling rivalry and allegiance. I experienced the Almighty's goodness when Mark sat cross-legged on our living floor and strummed an acoustic concert as our girls danced around him. I acknowledged the Author of Life's wisdom in giving us our free-spirited Lainey, my opposite, and our strong-willed

Faith, my stunt double. God had chosen each of us for this family, to rub up against one another and soften the rough edges.

The Third Yes

Mark finally did say yes to baby number three. His wasn't an enthusiastic "YES, let's do this!" but an "OK, if you want to." And that was plenty good enough for me. My poor husband frequently caved to my relentless hounding, but I knew—in the end—he would thank me.

I'm not bossy, I just knew what we should be doing, and I didn't mind commandeering the reins to head us in the right direction. (Of course, this self-justifying streak reflects an entirely unbiblical perspective that I'm sure I will have to answer for one day.)

So, we were going to have another baby. The next question, being that we were infertile and all, was: How would this baby find its way into our clan? For three years, we had left the door open for a natural pregnancy, but despite Dr. Dodds's sage advice to "make hay while the sun shined," Mark and I never conceived.

The obvious choice was adoption. After two successful adoptions, we were experts on the process and had an up-to-date home study and a reliable agency. But we couldn't ignore the cons to this approach, namely pinning our hopes on a birth mom who might not follow through with her plans—the sleepless nights, the wait and see, the birth-parent meetings reminiscent of the Spanish Inquisition. Sure, adoption would give us a child eventually, but we couldn't avoid the white-knuckle ride to the end.

A second option was another round of *in vitro*. Mark and I had survived three IVF procedures and a tubal pregnancy. I was *not* excited about filling my body with more mood-altering drugs, painful blood draws, prodding ultrasounds, and 48-hours sentenced to bed rest. Waiting two weeks for pregnancy test results was the worst part because it invited self-doubt and second-guessing. In sum, Mark and I had spent about 14 months tangled up in treatment cycles, and my only reward was a missing fallopian tube and carved-up abdomen. One more laparoscopic surgery and my belly button would unravel, rendering my drawer full of bikinis obsolete. It seemed that pursuing IVF anew would be an act of self-torture that still might not pay dividends.

Our last option was the one we had shoved to the backburner a year earlier: gestational surrogacy. When I had added it to the list of infertility options nine years earlier, the choice had seemed ripped from a sci-fi novel. The first traditional surrogacy arrangement had been conducted in America in 1980, but the practice remained far from common. And despite a handful of movies that had taken on the subject, I didn't know a single soul who had brought a baby into the world through a surrogate.

I had seen pictures of my own embryos in the petri dish and knew it was medically possible for people in white lab coats to unite sperm and egg beneath a microscope. What's more, Doctor Dodds had placed these microscopic blastocysts back into my womb for IVF. But the logistics of taking two women—biological mother and gestational carrier—from point A to point B mystified me.

Besides the complicated medical protocol, enlisting a surrogate would open a can of legal and emotional worms. Would it be weird to have another woman pregnant with our baby? What laws even governed those arrangements?

Adding to surrogacy's complicated logistics, it seemed everyone had an opinion on the ethical use of assistive reproductive technologies (ART). Mark and I—with our multiple IVF attempts—had long since spurned the need for *public* approval. On infertility and its treatments, there were few people whose opinions carried any weight. I would have loved to sit down at the feet of Jesus, like Martha's sister, Mary, had a couple thousand years ago, and pick his brain. I would have shared with him our surrogacy plans and asked if such a pursuit could be blessed.

However, in the year of our Lord 2006, I sought out wisdom where I could find it.

Plenty of Christian leaders had weighed in on the matter and none were lining up to support the practice due to surrogacy's seeming violation of the creation norm for marriage. God had created Adam and Eve who had then created Cain and Abel, no third party necessary. In the age of test-tube babies and donor eggs and sperm, we were a long way from the garden. Could a surrogacy arrangement still honor God's careful design?

More importantly, where could *I* begin to discern God's will on the topic for myself? Along with the Ten Commandments, I had always sifted my life choices through Christ's command to love God and love others. Did surrogacy violate God's laws or Jesus' teachings?

Of the Ten Commandments, the only one that seemed pertinent was the order not to commit adultery. Since adultery involved sexual relations outside of marriage, and doctors (not Mark) would impregnate Johnna via high-tech turkey baster, I quickly dismissed our culpability on this command. Further, a surrogacy arrangement did not jeopardize my love for God. On the contrary, moving forward would require me to trust his faithfulness—and his provision—absolutely.

The next question, though, was this: Could pursuing surrogacy unfairly take advantage of my neighbor, in this case Johnna? Certainly commercial surrogacy, where money is exchanged for the service of carrying a baby, could be considered human trafficking. The worst instances of CS involve First World couples who make agreements with Third World surrogates. Certainly, this type of surrogacy was a clear violation of the carrier's, and thus the baby's, human dignity.

I pondered our potential arrangement with Johnna in light of Christian counsel and God's Word. Ours was a gestational surrogacy plan by which doctors would carry out an IVF procedure to achieve pregnancy; we would not be brokering a deal for a baby. Moreover, *Johnna* had approached Mark and me about surrogacy, certain that God had placed in her the desire to carry our baby.

Even though I couldn't be sure that pursuing surrogacy was God's desire for us, I detected no red flags. And ultimately, I concluded that Johnna's sacrificial obedience and Mark's and my earnest seeking would glorify him.

These days, I spent hours chasing after my girls to protect them from things that, from their limited perspective, seemed like good ideas. That tantalizing electrical outlet inviting a poke from little fingers. That swimming pool shimmering in the sun. The red bouncy ball rolling into the path of a passing car. Each time my girls rushed toward these potential dangers, I scooped them into my arms and returned them to safety with a firm "No!" If pursuing surrogacy was somehow running away from God instead of toward him, I trusted that his love and protection would cover me, even if that meant that I too would hear a resounding "No."

The Proposal

For a year, Johnna and I saw each other weekly at church, but we hadn't discussed the idea of surrogacy since her initial offer. For all I knew, the past 12 months had made her think twice. People were pretty fickle. Yet of all the women who had offered up a place in their womb for our baby to grow, Johnna was the most fitting. She was a friend—yes—but we were not joined at the hip, and she was not related to us by blood, which was one of my conditions.

My mind raced with thoughts of how our cousin, sister-in-law, or mother would insert herself into our day-to-day child rearing once she had served as our gestational carrier. I imagined that her unsolicited opinions on everything from sleeping arrangements to formula brand or choice of preschool would spew forth without hesitation.

No, thank you. I had no desire to co-parent.

It was a bonus that Johnna and her husband, Steve, had two kiddos and no desire to add a third. If Johnna was still into this crazy idea, it was because of her passion to serve us, not a desire to play "Mom" to one more child.

Like Faith, our church plant—Crosswind Community—was in its toddlerhood. The congregation of eight to 10 had first met in basements then moved to a school gymnasium and was now a group of 200 worshiping in a bowling alley. Crosswind Community gave new meaning to the term "holy rollers," which passersby delighted in pointing out. Our setup team bustled in every Sunday at 7:00 a.m. to transform the smoky space into a sanctuary good and pleasing to God. When the crew had finished their preparations, our worship space mirrored the Sistine Chapel, except that our chancel was erected between ball returns and our fragrant incense smelled suspiciously like Febreze. Our mission was to "love the world into a growing relationship with Jesus Christ and to share His passion with the world," and everyone worked together to make it happen.

On a cold January day, after one of our services, I pulled Johnna aside to pop the question.

"We were just wondering," I began, "if your offer to carry a baby for us still stands."

I fiddled with the zipper tab on my coat, waiting for Johnna to equivocate. Instead she beamed. "Yes!"

I backpedaled. "You might want to think about it for a while and talk to Steve and the kids and then let us know," I advised. "There's a lot more to surrogacy than you might realize."

I was intimately familiar with the IVF procedure and figured Johnna would have to go through similar steps to get the two of us synced before embryo transfer. Johnna's steady gaze met mine.

"We talk about it all the time, and I've already gotten the all clear from my doctor. I'm ready to do it."

Since my warning about surrogacy's complications had fallen on deaf ears, I took a different tack.

"How about if you come with me to see my fertility specialist, we find out together what it's all about, and you make a decision from there?"

"Sounds good," she said, reaching into her purse to pull out a pocket-size calendar. "I'm free on Tuesdays. When do you want to do it?"

This Johnna woman clearly meant business.

"Um…I can schedule an appointment this week and get back to you?"

When Johnna learned the facts, her enthusiasm for carrying our baby would freeze over like tulips in one of Michigan's April snowstorms.

"OK," she chirped, "I can't wait!"

Then again, maybe not.

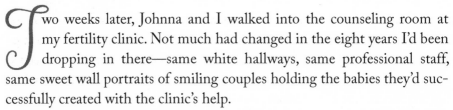

CHAPTER 19

Pitfalls & Pitches

*T*wo weeks later, Johnna and I walked into the counseling room at my fertility clinic. Not much had changed in the eight years I'd been dropping in there—same white hallways, same professional staff, same sweet wall portraits of smiling couples holding the babies they'd successfully created with the clinic's help.

Johnna and I followed Kathy, an ART nurse, into a small consulting room where we all took seats at a round table. Kathy plopped down a phone book in front of us. Oh wait, that was just the file chronicling my infertility saga.

"So, what brings the two of you here today?"

It had been four years since the miscarriage that followed Lainey's birth, so I filled Kathy in.

"We were wondering if you could tell us about surrogacy. Johnna is considering carrying a baby for us, and we would like to know what's involved."

Here we go, I thought, *the beginning of the end.*

Kathy handed us some forms from the file cabinet next to her and encouraged us to take notes as she talked.

"Since surrogacy is quite complicated, a lot of people leave here and can't remember a single thing." She laughed.

Ever the compliant student, I grabbed a pen from my purse to jot down relevant information, and Johnna smiled at me reassuringly.

"First of all," Kathy continued, "would Johnna be donating her eggs or are we going to be working with yours?"

"Oh! Well, with all the things that have gone wrong with my body, my eggs are actually OK. We'd be using mine, not anybody else's."

"OK," the nurse said. "Then we're not talking about surrogacy, where the carrier donates her egg. Johnna would be what's called a 'gestational carrier' or 'gestational surrogate.' She would carry and give birth to you and your husband's biological embryo." Kathy looked up from her notes for verification.

"Yes, exactly," I confirmed.

This was only an initial consultation, but my head was buzzing at the prospect of a baby with my blue eyes and Mark's dark wavy hair. Maybe we hadn't reached the statute of limitations on pursuing that pipe dream.

"The procedure itself will require synchronizing you and Johnna's menstrual cycles with birth control pills and daily injections of medicine to suppress ovulation. Then Johnna will take estrogen to ready her uterus, and you will be on injectable fertility meds again to stimulate follicle production."

So far so good. There wasn't anything in Kathy's explanation that I hadn't already done, but I wondered what was going on in Johnna's mind. She was a newbie to the world of making babies outside of the bedroom.

"During the drug regimen," Kathy went on, "we monitor your eggs and the thickness of Johnna's uterine lining using blood tests and trans-vaginal ultrasounds. Once everything looks good, you'll go through egg retrieval, just as you did with IVF, but this time, three to five days after the eggs have been retrieved and fertilized with your husband's sperm, the doctor will transfer the embryos to *Johnna's* uterus, instead of yours."

Kathy turned to Johnna.

"That procedure is much like a pap smear, Johnna, and you would stay lying down at the office for about an hour to give the embryos a chance to take hold."

I glanced over to see if Johnna's eyes had bugged out yet or if she was clutching her purse in preparation for a quick exit. She nodded at Kathy like the nurse was delivering a Tupperware spiel. Either Johnna was an excellent actress or she was truly unflappable.

"Any questions so far?"

Yes, actually. Dollar signs had popped into my mind when Kathy reeled off the double dose of prescribed meds, blood tests, ultrasounds, and embryo retrieval/transfer. IVF for one was a big-ticket item, and Mark and I had the home equity payment to prove it. It only made sense that adding another womb to the mix would mean twice the cost. Johnna had decent medical insurance through Steve's work, but I was certain that it wasn't going to cover infertility procedures.

Johnna would also be carrying a baby that didn't belong to her but receiving insurance benefits for prenatal care and hospital labor and delivery. Yo, Kathy, how exactly does that work?

"In our experience," she explained, "most insurance companies will pick up the cost of all of the lab work, blood tests, ultrasounds, etc., and the meds. However, they will not pay for the actual infertility procedures, which are the egg retrieval and the embryo transfer."

This didn't seem so bad. A non-surgical IVF would run to about $10,000. The cost would be considerably more if we were required to pay for tests and prescription drugs.

"You also need to know that paying someone to carry a baby is illegal in Michigan," Kathy cautioned.

Johnna snorted and shook her head.

"This is *my* dream," she told Kathy, though it was news to me too. "It's something God wants me to do. I would never expect payment to help Sarah out like this. Steve and I struggled for a few months to conceive, so I had a taste of how it feels. I just want to see Mark and Sarah have their baby."

I was dumbstruck. This was *her dream*? Aside from having a family, my dreams consisted of jetting to Italy to sip wine and nosh pasta and owning a big house so I could invite people over to sip wine and nosh pasta. I was certainly no Kim Kardashian, but I didn't spend much time searching outside myself to make someone else's dream come true.

But this was a business meeting, so I shook off my awe at Johnna's altruism and interjected.

"Mark and I would pay out of pocket for the IVF procedure, but between Johnna's policy and ours, the insurance will cover a good chunk."

Kathy looked back and forth, weighing her words.

"That's what we would hope for," she replied, "but you have to be prepared to cover *all* of the expenses if for some reason insurance doesn't."

Kathy was definitely leaving something out.

"And why would that happen?" I asked.

Kathy had a ready example. In one of the clinic's cases, an infertile woman's sister became her gestational carrier and carried the pregnancy successfully to term. The press got a hold of the story and crafted a human-interest segment that aired on the local news. The segment featured the two sisters, both Christians, sharing about the surrogacy experience and the healthy baby born as a result.

The sister who had served as the carrier happened to be the full-time employee of a prominent company in Grand Rapids. The news piece alerted the company's executives to the fact that their employee had been involved in a gestational carrier arrangement and that *their* company insurance plan had paid for the associated medications, blood work, and ultrasounds. The insurance plan had, of course, also paid for prenatal care and a hospital bill for labor and delivery. Because the company's leadership objected to gestational surrogacy on ethical grounds, they sued their employee to recover their costs. And they won.

When Kathy wrapped up her report on the lawsuit, I shook my head in disbelief. The mean-spiritedness of a few wealthy "Christian" CEOs had floored me. These executives had likely never wanted for a child but demanded restitution for an infertility procedure they didn't understand instead of rejoicing in the life created by it. Their harsh denouncement of surrogacy made me wary of similar judgment from my brothers and sisters in Christ. Were we prepared to gracefully defend our decision if we chose to move forward? More importantly, could Mark and I live with the clash between mainstream evangelical thought and our own prayerfully reached conclusion on surrogacy?

The sisters' story also made me worry about the additional debt Mark and I would incur if the insurance companies, or our employers, turned on us. What if there were complications? What if a C-section or lengthy hospital stay was necessary? If Steve's employer or mine got nosy and objected to a gestational carrier arrangement, we could be socked with enough bills to put our great grandchildren in the poorhouse. However unlikely it was, insurance coverage could technically be yanked out from under our feet. My budget-conscious husband would not fail to take this concern into account. Of all the factors that could throw a wrench into our plans, the inability to predict surrogacy's cost was the one that might prevent us from signing on the dotted line.

But Kathy was just getting started. Along with the demanding medical procedure, the expense, and the potential complications of involving two insurance companies, there was the legal aspect of surrogacy.

While the technology for IVF and surrogacy had been around for over 20 years, the laws related to such cases weren't exactly up to date . Science could create an embryo *ex utero* and place it in a third party, but the law had made minimal steps in governing the relationships around the resulting baby. At the time, Kathy told us, there was only one lawyer in Michigan who handled the mountains of paperwork generated by a gestational surrogacy. Luckily, our clinic referred patients to this lawyer. Unluckily, his office was three hours away, and he didn't work for free.

Surrogacy was entirely too complicated and expensive, and I had begun to plan our escape when my old friend Dr. Dodds burst through the door.

"Sorry I'm late!" he announced cheerfully, shaking my hand and introducing himself to Johnna before he joined our roundtable.

"How are things going here? Do you have any questions?"

Dr. Dodds's genuine smile had always quelled my doubts during infertility treatment.

I spilled the beans.

"Well, I'm feeling pretty overwhelmed. Going through the procedure *again*, the cost, the insurance, the legal channels—it all just feels impossible. I don't know if I can do it."

Dr. Dodds leaned toward me, elbows on the table, as I shared my fears. I was 36 years old, and Mark was 39. In the past decade, we had spent scads of our time, energy, and financial resources chasing after baby dreams. This attempt to have a biological child would be the end of the line. I had to make peace with whatever decision Mark and I made and then slam and bolt the door.

We *could* try for one more IVF attempt on our own with only my unreliable reproductive system in play. Keeping Johnna out of the process would bypass the mess of one more medical chart, one more womb. Or we could go with Johnna, assuming she was still willing, and trust God to slay the monsters lurking around every corner. Of course, we could also abandon the idea of a third little Rollandini and embrace the freedom of a completed family of four, of being settled and satisfied—just like Mark had entreated me so many times to be.

Since decision-making is not my strong suit and our future family was at stake, I passed the buck to Dr. Dodds.

"What would you do if you were in my shoes?"

Dr. Dodds's handsome face grew pensive as he sat back in the chair and stroked his stubbly chin. Then his eyes locked onto mine with the intensity of a street-corner evangelist.

"You've been through a lot," he said softly. "If this is the last time you're going through treatment…I'd go with Johnna."

He turned his head a fraction to level his gaze at Johnna.

"You're Sarah and Mark's very best chance," he said, "and I'll do my best to bring them a baby."

When we left the office, Johnna bubbled with excitement, on board with being a gestational carrier, despite its pitfalls. I, however, was still weighing the glut of information in my head, framing it for my discussion with Mark. My husband was a black-and-white kind of guy. If the possible cons outweighed the pros, his final answer would be a resounding, "No." I pulled into Johnna's driveway and gave her a grateful hug with a promise to call soon.

"It's all going to work out!" she promised before bouncing toward the front door.

I shifted the minivan into reverse and backed out of the driveway. I had exactly six minutes to prepare my sales pitch for Mark. I wished I had Johnna's faith.

The Pitch

Lainey and Faith were tucked safely into bed before I broached the subject in our living room scattered with board books and baby dolls. I shot to tell

Mark the whole truth as I reviewed my copious notes. Although tempted to share only the benign parts of the surrogacy process and leave out the alarming possibility of a lawsuit, my husband deserved full disclosure. I had no desire to go through the emotional ride of IVF essentially on my own with Mark acting as the begrudging sperm donor.

Sitting on the floor crisscross-applesauce, I channeled my nervous energy into matching a basket of socks as I delivered my report. Mark, also a multitasker, recovered the girls' playthings and returned them to their proper shelves and bins.

I braced myself for Mark's resistance. As I suspected, the possibility of a grievous financial burden gave him pause.

"We're talking about tens of thousands of dollars here," Mark exhorted. "We'd be in debt until the kids are out of the house!"

To be fair, if Johnna didn't get pregnant, Mark and I would only be stuck with the expenses of egg retrieval and transfer, around $10,000, a risk we could afford to take. If Johnna *did* get pregnant, we could hope that Steve's employer and his insurance company wouldn't get curious. Kathy had been obligated to tell us the worst-case scenario. Yes, counting on insurance coverage was a gamble, but the odds were in our favor. If Johnna's insurance got pulled, whatever bills we incurred would pale in comparison to the value of having another child.

There's no doubt my emotional logic was not Dave Ramsey-approved, but *fiddle-dee-dee*, I couldn't have cared less.

I sensed an urgency to win Mark over before he delivered his verdict.

"What is twenty or thirty thousand dollars to us in ten years?" I cried.

In lieu of surrogacy, would our money be prudently stuffed into savings or stocks? Spent on Disney World or Friday nights at Chuck-E-Cheese? How about a nice new Honda Odyssey paid for in cash? Whatever our hard-earned coins could purchase in fun or financial security, the economic reward of our fiscal responsibility could never rival the wonder of having our baby.

I could see myself in 10 years as clearly as I saw myself today, and the question of *"Why didn't we just try it?"* would hound me even as I tried to kick it to the curb. I feared the regret would drive a wedge of bitterness between my husband and me.

"OK…let's give it one last shot," I heard Mark say.

Yes. My husband said, "Yes," one more time to his intractable wife.

I thanked God for his grace in spite of my bent toward rebellion. While I would likely never attain the virtue of biblical submission, Mark had certainly plumbed the depths of a Christ-like love for his bride.

Overwhelmed, I threw my arms around my husband and planted kisses up and down his face. Mark gave me half a smile along with a parental look that said, "*Settle down now.*" Then I made a beeline for the phone. I was sure Johnna would pick up on the first ring.

The Legal Stuff

Our next step was to take Johnna and Steve to meet with the lawyer and give them one final opportunity to back out. Thankfully, because it was lake-effect snow season in West Michigan, Eric the lawyer made the three-hour trek from Traverse City on slippery roads to meet with us in the conference room of our local library. He was a distinguished gentleman in a charcoal suit and power tie who was graying around the temples.

I knew little about attorneys, but Eric would've fit perfectly into any number of Hollywood courtroom dramas. I imagined Jack Nicholson from *A Few Good Men* shouting from the witness stand, "You can't handle the truth!" while Eric gazed back unaffectedly.

After everyone was introduced, Eric pulled some files from his leather briefcase, spread them out on the table, and went on to explain the legal aspects of gestational surrogacy. The gist of it was this: With written consent, Eric would file a "pre-birth order" with our county of residence, which would allow our names, rather than Johnna's and Steve's, to be placed on the baby's birth certificate in the hospital. This order would clarify who the baby's biological parents were and give Mark and me full custodial rights from minute one.

Eric made the process sound simple. However, he cautioned that most of his clients had been from the more densely populated east side of the state. There, surrogacy arrangements were, if not common, at least more ordinary than in Southwest Michigan. Unlike the cosmopolitan suburbs of Detroit, West Michigan was known for its staunchly conservative values and resistance to change. The approval of the pre-birth order rested solely on the shoulders of whichever county judge's desk the file fell upon. And if the judge were suspicious of new-fangled technologies, he would likely turn down our request. It was ironic that living in this neck of the woods—the perfect place to raise a family—could hurt our case.

Walking out of the library, we asked Johnna and Steve to consider the legal dimension of gestational surrogacy and get back to us. They replied without hesitation.

"What are we waiting for? Let's do it!"

After all of the legal speak Mark and I were a little shaky. Steve and Johnna, on the other hand, continued to be fearless. Even with the prospect of turning over their medical records and undergoing a psychological screening test, they were all in. In addition, Johnna was prepared to undergo the sonohystogram (HSG) and mock embryo transfer (ET) tests to check the condition of her uterus.

All that was left was to sign the contract Eric had presented and forward it to the clinic. Our four signatures would start the ball rolling toward the two-cycle regimen that led right up to retrieval and transfer.

Over the past month, I had unleashed on Johnna and Steve all the scary little details of a gestational-carrier arrangement. They had responded by batting these facts away like gnats. Despite my attempts at freaking Johnna out, she had stood firm. And for his part, Steve pledged to support his wife through the aches, pains, and marital strain of pregnancy, with zero payoff for him. Now it was time to share our unconventional game plan with our support network. We needed their prayers and encouragement for this road we were determined to travel. I only hoped they would share our enthusiasm.

CHAPTER 20

The Heartbeat & the Holy Spirit

Once our procedure was officially on the clinic's calendar, Johnna and I became close confidants almost overnight. It was March. We wouldn't start the process of getting our systems in sync for another month, but the goal of making a baby hung out there like a carrot around which our lives revolved. Johnna and I shopped, scrapbooked, and gathered our families together for Sunday pot roast and Uno. Many of our chats began with, "If we're pregnant by then…" or, "If the baby is due in winter…" I knew that I hung my hopes on a procedure that gave us a 50/50 chance of a biological child, but it was impossible to brush aside the possibility.

Mark and I gradually shared our plans with our parents and a few close friends who lent a curious brand of support. The first question on everyone's mind was, "Won't it be hard for Johnna to carry a baby only to give it up? What if she changes her mind?"

Our tribe's understanding of a "surrogate" (as everyone called Johnna despite my efforts to shift their language to "gestational carrier") was limited to movies and sensationalist news stories that ended in custody battles between surrogate and biological parents. And while our friends admired Johnna's altruism, they were secretly suspicious of some ulterior motive and eager for a face-to-face meeting to assuage their fears. I couldn't knock their skepticism; it's where I had been just weeks earlier.

To clear up these doubts, Johnna suggested a pre-embryo-transfer question-and-answer session with my mom. On a warm day in April, just after Johnna and I had begun our medications, we plopped in a circle of lawn chairs on my parents' cedar deck. The smell of hyacinth and rain was in the air as the robins reminded us to "cheer up, cheer up." We sipped lemonade and nibbled on cheese and crackers as Mom kept the conversation smooth and polite.

Johnna, ever the pragmatist, cut to the chase.

"I heard you have some questions, so fire away!"

Mom raised her eyebrows and laughed.

"Well," my mom began, fiddling with her gold necklace, "I have no problem with the procedure itself, or the use of IVF, but how do you know that after the baby comes, you won't want to keep it?"

Johnna and I exchanged knowing glances.

This was the question we had fielded over and over again, along with acerbic comments from women of childbearing age, like, *"Being a surrogate is OK for her, but I could never give up a baby I carried for nine months!"* These thoughtless remarks were a way of patting Johnna on the back for her humanitarian display of selflessness while simultaneously slapping her in the face. The insinuation was that Johnna must be off her rocker to consider carrying a baby for another woman.

I was privy to the same sentiment when Mark and I were matched with our girls' birth moms. Even though adoption was a different scenario, such cavalier judgments made me cringe every time. Couldn't the fertile world dump their philosophizing and recognize these women's sacrifices as divine gifts? The world was in short supply of women stepping forward to help the fertility-challenged, and I found their armchair quarterbacking maddening.

But Mom's angle was one of genuine concern. What if we achieved a pregnancy only to have Johnna change her mind when the *actual* baby arrived? The real question for my mom wasn't how could *anyone* do it but could *Johnna?* Was she sincere and grounded enough to follow through with our plan? Had she counted the physical and emotional costs of carrying a baby she would not bring home from the hospital?

Johnna responded without equivocation, as she had when faced with this same question from our friends at church.

"If this baby was Steve's and mine, I absolutely could not do it, but we're talking about Sarah and Mark's baby here. I see myself as an incubator. The baby is going to look like Sarah and Mark, not my kids, because it'll be made from the two of them. This baby will not be *mine*."

My mom nodded slowly.

And then, lightening the mood in typical fashion, Johnna added, "Besides, I can barely handle my own two kids; I do *not* want another!"

We all chuckled at her candor, but Johnna spoke the truth. She was a good mom to Zach and Cassidy, but she was no Michelle Duggar. Two kids was her limit.

Hanging out with Johnna, I'd learned that she was as straightforward and self-effacing as she appeared to be. My mom picked up the same lesson that day. Johnna's compassion came as naturally to her as my ambition. In a society in which most people looked out for number one, Johnna gladly gave up her heart to follow where God's led, and she didn't stop to weigh the pros and cons. She wasn't perfect, but the way she humbled herself for others—for me—was the very heart of Christ.

Getting in Sync

Johnna and my intricate reproductive systems got synced without a hitch, but there was a slight hiccup with Mark's schedule. My eggs were ripe and Johnna's uterus raring to go in early May, just as Mark was headed out of state on a motor-coach full of high-spirited high schoolers. As an assistant principal and Washington, D.C. expert, he would chaperone the annual senior trip to our nation's capital and miss the egg retrieval and embryo transfer in the process. Consequently, the clinic froze Mark's sperm sample days before the procedure to preserve their viability; those wiggly X and Y chromosomes would meet their date with destiny as Mark played tour guide 700 miles away.

It was my third time through the painful process of egg retrieval and this time Johnna would be the one to hold my hand and fill me in on my drug-induced misconduct. Again, I tried to kick the embryologist and ranted about a co-worker with whom I had no quarrel when in my right mind.

It had been six years since our last IVF attempt, and my normally plentiful eggs had become lackluster with age. When Johnna and I showed up for the transfer a few days later, Dr. Dodds apologized that out of the five eggs retrieved and fertilized, only two embryos had continued to develop. Three had always been our magic number, the one that gave us a significant chance of pregnancy.

Up until transfer day, I had been optimistic. We had a stellar womb that had delivered two babies, and my eggs had always held up their end of the bargain. Now, with only two embryos to transfer, our chances of achieving a pregnancy had dimmed.

Dr. Dodds launched into a pep talk.

"I know we were hoping to have more embryos," he said, "but the two that we have are of excellent quality, and it only takes one!"

I nodded my head, unable to get words out.

Embryo grading is based on cell quality. The goal is to have cells of equal size with minimal fragmentation. You don't want to have parts of the embryo going rogue and separating from the nucleated portion of the cell.

Dr. Dodds's embryo report could've been my first parent-teacher conference. On a scale of 1–4, my little blastocysts were a 2+. Our pre-born kids were solid students but had room for improvement. *Maybe,* I thought, *two will be our magic number.*

After Dr. Dodds's report, Johnna shrugged on her hospital gown and assumed the same position I had taken two days earlier. It was a surreal switcheroo as Johnna lay back on the table, feet up in the stirrups, and I held *her* hand while Dr. Dodds completed the quick embryo transfer. I observed the procedure from the head of the bed while I visualized our two embryos slowly emerging from the end of the catheter into Johnna's rich uterus. I imagined the round cells floating weightlessly, like bubbles, at first and then rolling downhill like microscopic boulders in an alien landscape, stirring up debris until they gently came to rest. A double cocoon attached to Johnna's insulated womb.

In truth, the placement of our embryos was not by chance. Johnna's uterus had been measured precisely and the location for transfer selected months before. But this imagery helped me to connect with the part of Mark and me that was now outside of myself and, therefore, outside of my control.

With the transfer complete, a nurse wheeled Johnna to a curtained recovery area where she would lie flat for a couple hours. Instead of rushing off, Dr. Dodds stayed to chat and crack jokes. I saw his presence in the waiting room as part of his mission in "Operation Baby Rollandini," and it soothed my worry.

Dr. Dodds was a believer whose profession drew him behind the curtain of God's covert workings. After handling the delicate process of egg retrieval and embryo transfer, even the good doctor had to offer up the outcome to heaven.

When it was time to leave, Johnna rolled out of the hospital bed as I prayed furiously for our budding embryos to stay put. I continued my petitions on the drive to Panera as Johnna reclined in the passenger seat of our minivan. I slowed at every stoplight and gentled around each turn to guard the fragile, floating life inside her.

Pulling into the parking lot, I asked for Johnna's order. We had decided to pick up lunch to-go so she could lie down for a few more precious minutes.

"I'll have a ham and cheese and a Diet Coke," she said.

A Diet Coke? It took every fiber of my being not to launch into a lecture about the vices of diet soda. How could she guzzle aspartame with my babies on the inside? *My* order for Johnna would have included an organic mixed greens salad, whole grain sandwich, and spring water. Whereas I cooked 99% of our meals at home with fresh and healthy ingredients, Johnna was hopeless in the kitchen. Many of the Garretts' dinners consisted of burgers and fries in disposable containers. Our family reserved soft drinks for parties, as a special treat. The carbonated beverage was the staple of Johnna's clan.

The last several months, I had been immersed in the process of achieving a pregnancy and hadn't thought much past that accomplishment, but standing in line at Panera with the smell of fresh sourdough and the clatter of trays around me, I had an epiphany. My daughters had arrived with only a few months' preparation, and I'd had little time or right to question their birth mom's prenatal choices.

This time, our babies could spend the next nine months residing in Johnna's belly, and I could spend that time worrying about the minutiae of her choices. Fast food and diet sodas, appropriate sleeping positions, and even frequency and method of sex popped uninvited onto the whiteboard of my mind. I quickly erased these images before delivering Johnna her order and flashing my best game show host smile.

"Here's your Diet Coke," I said through gritted teeth.

My babies were guests in a foreign land, the space between us as vast and unyielding as the Sahara desert. Johnna's love for Diet Coke was likely the smallest of many preferences different from my own, and, like so many things in the world of infertility, I would have to learn to let it go.

The Eleventh Hour

A few days post-transfer, I slouched in the dim sanctuary of our bowling alley church overwhelmed. The 11:00 service was over, as was my ability to control anything about our last attempt at pregnancy. I stared down at the neon, confetti-printed carpet contemplating the likelihood of another negative test result. I blinked back tears, and the confetti blurred. I was alone and afraid.

I couldn't settle my thoughts enough to pray, but Jesus showed up anyway. Suddenly, I was filled with a calm that transcended my desire for a positive pregnancy test. *I will never abandon you,* he reminded me. Whatever God's final answer to our 11th hour effort, we were going to be OK.

That night, as I lay in bed, I opened my Bible to the verse listed in my evening devotional. Reading the Scripture, I was once again hit with a wave of assurance. The words from Psalm 113 were another personal memo from my God: "He gives the barren woman a home, making her the joyous mother of children. Praise the Lord!" It was a reminder and also a promise. *I came through for you before, and I will again.* The Lord had already removed mountains from my path; it was time for me to stop playing at trust and raise my Ebenezer stone in recognition of his faithfulness. No more childish demands that balanced my belief upon the shaky precipice of prayers answered in my timing and by my design. God was either good or he wasn't…and he was. No pregnancy test, positive or negative, would change that.

Romance & Revelation

It was a Thursday. We only had four days until the blood test at the clinic, and Johnna was hosting a Positively Romance party, a home sales company that specialized in bath, beauty, and bedroom products promising to enhance a couple's intimacy. It was, perhaps, the only type of home party in which husbands eagerly handed their wives a Visa card on the way out the door and told them to max it out.

Never mind that Johnna was on doctor's orders to refrain from such intimacy. The gathering was just an excuse to get some girlfriends together and laugh until they cried. At least, that's what I told myself to keep from wagging my finger at Johnna and reminding her about the "no sex 'til the test" rule.

Johnna had called earlier in the day to ask for help with setup .

Setup? I thought. *What exactly needs to be set up?*

I'd attended loads of home parties before and also hosted a few. Mostly, women just sat around in the living room nibbling hors d'oeuvres and gabbing while the sales lady unfurled her wares. Oh, well. Maybe Johnna needed help getting the food ready. Either way, I couldn't exactly say no with Johnna offering up her uterus for the next nine months. Mark agreed to keep the girls occupied for the evening, and I dashed off to the Garretts' to make myself useful.

It was unusually warm for late May. Michigan winters often lasted well into spring, and the sensation of sun and air on skin long covered by layers was delicious. Johnna greeted me at the door, all smiles, and we hugged as she invited me into her living room. The temperature outside had just grazed 70 degrees, but every fan in the house was going and Johnna's face glistened with sweat. Yes, she was glowing, I thought dryly.

Apart from the hum of fans, it was strangely quiet for a house with two little kids running around.

"Zack and Cassidy are playing over at the Mattinglys'," Johnna said breezily. "I'll put you to work in the kitchen."

After giving me instructions, she rushed off, and I got busy slicing marble jack cheese and arranging crackers prettily on plates.

I was about to cut into a block of Swiss when I heard Johnna calling from another part of the house.

"Coming!" I shouted, striding into the empty living room. "Where are you?"

"I'm in here," she yelled from the bathroom.

Did she need me to clean the toilet? When I walked in, Johnna stood facing me, one hand propped jauntily on the sink.

"What's up?" I inquired. "Am I on bathroom duty? Where's your toilet brush?"

Johnna smirked and handed me a thermometer. Was she sick? When I looked down at the grey stick, a word in bold black print stared back at me: PREGNANT.

"What!" I stammered. "What did you do?"

Johnna laughed before telling me the story.

"I knew how stressed out you were about waiting for the blood test, and I thought I could make you feel better if we got the results a little bit sooner," she explained. "That's why I invited you over here early. I had to tell you!"

Johnna raised her eyebrows cockily, as if to say, "I told you so," and waited for my reaction.

I shook off my shock and grabbed Johnna into an enthusiastic bear hug. We both laughed and cried as I held the magic wand out in front of us. I half expected its letters to disappear or for the word "not" to materialize next to the word "pregnant." I darted my eyes away from and then back to the wand to confirm that I wasn't hallucinating.

"I can't believe it. I really can't. Is there any other reason the stick would show you're pregnant if you're not?"

I was in denial big time, searching for any plausible argument to support a positive test besides the obvious reason of an actual pregnancy.

Johnna chuckled and shook her head at me. She was not even the least bit exasperated with my lack of faith, just amused.

"Nope, no other reason!" she responded. "The test says 'pregnant' because I am!"

I checked the clock. 6:45. Guests would be showing up any minute and, though some friends were aware of Operation Make-a-baby, we had kept most in the dark.

"OK." I sighed, gathering my thoughts. "Can we just keep this little news to ourselves until we talk to Dr. Dodds after Monday's blood test?"

"Sure, sorry if I threw you off. I just couldn't wait."

She looked like she'd been busted for running a red light.

Clearly, Johnna's empathy meter was off the charts. I should've realized that her agreement to carry our baby would involve not just housing a developing infant but shouldering my worry and impatience as well. The impromptu pregnancy test had veered from doctor's orders, but it was a welcome surprise.

Johnna and I spent the better part of the two-hour soiree with goofy smiles glued to our faces, casting covert glances at one another like partners in crime. And in a way, we *had* gone a bit Thelma and Louise. After Mark and I had tried for nearly 10 years, Johnna and I had hit a homerun the first time at bat and with Mark nearly 700 miles away. Johnna had also broken the rules with her early pregnancy test stunt. I'd long thought of her as a meek and mild Christian girl, but clearly she was a rebel in sheep's clothing.

With that in mind, I wagged my finger at her before walking out the door.

"Absolutely no 'positively romance' for you and Steve tonight, Johnna. Let's keep those babies in position until we get the all clear."

The Ultrasound

The blood test a few days later confirmed what Johnna already knew. She was, or rather we were, pregnant. With the official word from the clinic, we celebrated again while I anticipated our next step, an early ultrasound to listen for heartbeats and determine the number of babies, with trepidation. I secretly hoped for twins, which would fulfill our premarital dreams of raising a family of six and put to rest my incessant petitioning for more.

Despite the challenges of leaving his elementary students without their principal for the afternoon, Mark refused to miss the ultrasound appointment, though he may have questioned the wisdom of spending the afternoon with Johnna and me.

On the car ride, the two of us were in hysterics as we discussed how to account for our constant togetherness, especially as Johnna started to show. After having a "not that there's anything wrong with that" moment, Johnna and I agreed to avoid over-explaining our relationship to sheer strangers. They didn't need to know.

As a veteran "infertile," the "need to know" rule came in handy in a variety of situations, like pushing the cart in the produce aisle with two-year-old Lainey and newborn Faith when curious shoppers approached.

"Oh, she's so little…how old is she?" they would ask.

"Just two weeks," I replied, basking in their admiration.

The look of surprise. "Wow! You look so good!" they would gush, remarking on my post-pregnancy bod.

The pause to consider: To tell the abridged version of my story or not to tell?

"Thank you!" I beamed.

As my mom frequently reminded me, my pre-pregnancy figure was one small perk of infertility.

I was jittery as Mark, Johnna, and I entered the clinic that day. Thus far, my early ultrasounds had ended in tears and, later, cramping and blood. Mark and I waited outside the exam room while Johnna slipped into her gown then called us in as she hopped spryly onto the exam table. *Woah, easy with the hopping*, I thought.

Taking in the small, stark room with its bulky ultrasound machine, my palms felt clammy and the undertow of déjà vu threatened to suck me under. *Where was the doctor?*

Mark and I sat in the corner chairs while Johnna swung her bare legs like a pediatric patient, her attempt to cut through the tension. She knew about the agony of waiting here, how I relived the moments when the doctor broke the news, twice. *I'm sorry, there's no heartbeat.*

"Hey," she said, trying to snap me out of it, "It's going to be ok."

I smiled half-heartedly. *Thanks for trying.*

I pictured the square, black-and-white photo of my embryos taken on transfer day nearly four weeks earlier. Two separate, multi-cell bubbles surrounded by halo-like outer rings. I reminded myself to breathe. *Come on, you guys,* I entreated. *You can do this.* Then the only prayer that came to mind: *Please, please, please.*

Dr. Dodds rushed in, apologizing for his tardiness. The clock read only five minutes past appointment time. Not exactly late, but the empathic doctor appreciated the significance of this appointment. His eyebrows knit together and frown lines surfaced as he scrubbed his hands in the sink then yanked paper towels from the wall dispenser.

My heart thudded and then sped up. I stepped quickly to the head of the table and grabbed Johnna's hand as she lay back. Mark sidled up and grabbed mine. Dr. Dodds swiftly prepped Johnna for the procedure and plunged in the probe. I forgot to breathe.

Dr. Dodds's face lit up suddenly. "There it is!" he announced.

I had seen my own vacant uterus on screen enough times to know the glory of the image before me. The black almond shape of Johnna's uterus floated center screen. Attached at the top right quadrant was a grainy white blob enclosing a smaller black blob. Before I could entertain second guesses, Dr. Dodds spun the volume knob with his left hand and we witnessed the sweet sloshing gallop of a tiny heartbeat. Our baby.

The screen blurred as my eyes welled up with tears at the sight and sound of this long-awaited miracle. I bent down and gave Johnna an awkward hug.

"We did it!" I congratulated her.

"We sure did," she agreed, wiping away her own tears.

My eyes met Mark's, and I leaned into him as he wrapped me in a one-armed hug of solidarity and celebration.

"Looks like just the one," Dr. Dodds broke in as he jockeyed around the wand. "Yep, one healthy baby with a strong heartbeat! Considering the May transfer date, I'm going to put your estimated date of delivery at February seventeenth."

We had a due date! I watched everyone's posture relax as we breathed sighs of joyous relief. With the ultrasound complete, Mark and I headed back into the hallway to let Johnna dress. When she appeared in the hallway a moment later, Mark rewarded her with a high five and a hug.

With the sight and sound of our baby's beating heart, I could shelve my worry for the time being. It was time to share our extraordinary news with the world, or at least the small group of champions who had been waiting to breathe right along with us.

Announcements & Old Shoes

Mark and I brought our parents up to speed with a simple phone call. Priority number one then became sharing the news with my grandparents before we broke the story to the rest of our circle. The world would have to wait until our first trimester was safely behind us.

My Grandma and Grandpa Westfield and Grandma Sisson were in their eighties, and we'd held back from sharing our pregnancy plans to avoid confusion should the procedure amount to nil. Since infertility had never enabled Mark and me to surprise our family with a pregnancy announcement, I seized this last opportunity to get creative.

I bought a couple of "Grandchild" frames at Hobby Lobby and stuck one of our early ultrasound pictures in each. The second weekend in June, we gathered at my parents' house for a summer barbecue, and Mark and I presented the framed pictures to my grandparents over apple pie. We waited for the delighted shock, the belly laughter, and the hearty congratulations. Instead, the octogenarians exchanged looks of consternation before uttering polite thank yous and returning to their pies à la mode.

To my aging grandparents, the ultrasound photo likely resembled a piece of modern art, and they had missed the point altogether. Sensing their confusion, Mom and I launched into a loud and lengthy explanation of this complicated pregnancy. When we had wrapped up, my dear grandparents nodded their heads in befuddled approval, and Mom and I were ready for a couple of stiff drinks. My "big reveal" moment had gone over like a lead balloon, another misadventure in our baby-making saga.

At our next family gathering, I brought Johnna rather than gimmicks. She sat around the table with my grandparents in the heat of the afternoon, sharing lunch in my parents' garage-come-veranda. The four of them laughed and swapped stories as the ceiling fan delivered a steady click-click. Having Johnna present at the table put flesh and blood on the surrogate pregnancy we had announced to my grandparents weeks earlier. Surrogacy was strange. Johnna was not.

When Johnna went home, Grandpa Westfield approached me, smiling. "That Johnna...she's like an old shoe."

My grandpa was a man's man who had spent his growing-up years in the Great Depression. A fellow of few words, especially when it came to compliments, Grandpa had offered a glowing endorsement. It was his way of saying I could trust Johnna and, though he might not fully understand this pregnancy, he was A-OK with my baby being carried by someone of her character.

Thwarting the Thief

On July 6, at six weeks, we had our last ultrasound at the infertility clinic. What had appeared as a blob just four weeks earlier was now clearly a baby, with arm buds, leg buds, an alien-like head, the sloping outline of a face, and a developing brain. This appointment was a huge milestone since it was the last we would spend at our infertility clinic. Johnna was being released to the care of her own OB/GYN, Dr. Menapace, and Mark and I were going with her.

We had what was now considered a "normal" pregnancy, with no known risk factors and no more progesterone shots. It was a mountaintop we'd forever scrabbled to reach, and I wanted to stick a flag in the dirt and call it good. Unfortunately, years of disappointment—when the idea of our baby had sprouted only to be cut off before harvest—held me back.

With about five weeks left in our first trimester, I found myself more consumed with worry than ever. Even with a normal pregnancy, there was a lengthy list of potential complications, and I considered every one. And unlike most expectant moms, I lacked the hormonal security blanket of "feeling" pregnant. It might be crazy to whine about missing out on morning sickness, fatigue, frequent trips to the bathroom, and tender breasts, but for me, these pregnancy side effects were welcome reminders that the life inside was growing safe and sound.

Fortunately, since our first trimester occurred in the summertime when school was out, I had plenty of time to grill Johnna for information. On sweltering July afternoons, we perched in lawn chairs in the front yard soaking our feet in the kiddie pool while Lainey, Faith, Cassidy, and Zach darted through the sprinklers' frigid spray.

"How are you feeling today?" I would ask, followed by, "Are you having any cravings? Still feeling sick? Are you tired? Do you think you should take a nap?"

Though tempted, I stopped short of requesting an intercourse schedule for my meticulous records.

Johnna was patient with my constant inquiries and generous with reporting, and I experienced remarkable calm in her presence. By midsummer, she sported a small baby bump that hitched her shirts catawampus and diverted my restlessness to the reality of our growing baby.

The minute Johnna and I were apart, however, a familiar anxiety crept back in, pillaging my peace. In the middle of joy, the thief had come to steal and kill and destroy, and I had stumbled right into his trap. Frankly, I was sick to death of it. The constant roiling stomach, the badgering thoughts that warned of certain doom crouched on every corner.

These lies stole not only my present—the only thing I could hold in my hands—but my hope for the future. I was in serious need of a rescue that could not be found in Amazon's warehouses of self-help books or in the skills I'd gained from therapy. The only way to scrap my worry was to throw myself headlong into a constant conversation with the great comforter, the Holy Spirit.

True confession: I am not a good pray-er. Often, a root canal seems more inviting than spending time in actual quiet talking to God and listening for his voice. I spent much of my prayer time detailing my fears— miscarriage, prematurity, congenital defect, stillbirth—and my mind often wandered into grocery and to-do lists. With my antsy appeals to God, I was thankful for the steadiness, the downright dependability, of the Holy Spirit's eloquent cries.

These prayers became my lifeline, a chanting doxology that installed God in his rightful place in my cluttered mind.

CHAPTER 21

Cosmo

*A*long with the technology that had helped engineer our pregnancy—ultrasound, egg retrieval, intracytoplasmic sperm injection, and embryo transfer—the ART team had presented Mark and me with the option of choosing our baby's sex.

We'd hashed over this choice months before our IVF attempt. Since the doctors and embryologists would already be fiddling with our DNA in a petri dish, why not have them handpick the boy sperm so we could round out our family with a son?

The option was tempting. Aside from the sperm-sorting price tag of around $2,000, though, choosing our baby's sex felt like meddling in God's business a bit too much. The IVF procedure had already disrupted the natural process of baby making, and we'd made a tentative peace with it. Sperm-sorting felt manipulative—even selfish. We had trusted God to bring us our daughters and resolved to leave baby number three's gender up to him as well.

On September 28, 2006, Steve, Johnna, Mark, and I trooped into Dr. Menapace's office for our official 20-week ultrasound. This so-called "anomaly scan" was a routine ultrasound to confirm that the baby was developing normally. The 30-minute scan would allow the sonographer to identify the baby's heartbeat and body parts and to share its sex, if we were curious. The Rollandini basement was occupied by Rubbermaid tubs brimming with pastels, ruffles, and lace. We wanted to know.

Because our baby's genetic makeup consisted of egg and sperm derived from 36- and 39-year-old parents, Dr. Menapace's office had recommended other screening tests weeks earlier. Amniocentesis and the triple test would detect chromosomal abnormalities, the most common of which is Down Syndrome. These tests were optional, and, with Johnna's OK, Mark and I declined them.

With infertility treatments, Mark and I had witnessed the first hours of life grasping for its place in the world. We were also keenly aware that our daughters' birth mothers could have chosen convenience over conscience and left this universe with two gaping holes. Trying to conceive had skimmed the fat from human arguments and left us with this boiled down truth: All life is of inestimable value. If doctors identified genetic issues in our baby at any point, there was no question Johnna would carry the pregnancy to term.

The ultrasound tech bustled into the closet-sized room to find Johnna on the table and the rest of us crowded around her like groupies. I glanced at the tech, hoping she was in the mood to chat. Getting a tech with an attitude could put a damper on the free sharing of information. Today, however, we had a winner.

Kim, a petite brunette, greeted us and politely asked for the context of our story. Apparently four adults in their late 30s are not representative of your typical ultrasound audience.

Voicing her support for our group effort, Kim squeezed the warmed gel onto the ultrasound wand and began to glide over the crest of Johnna's baby bump as we peered at the small screen. The grainy triangle brightened with black and white confetti until it came to rest on the iridescent outline of a baby. I no longer needed an expert to help me decipher the bony arc of a spinal cord. Mark grabbed my hand, and I swiveled away from the screen to catch a glimpse of my husband. His neck was craned forward, mouth open.

Kim maneuvered the wand a few inches to the left.

"Do we want to know the sex?" she asked with a hint of amusement.

"Umm, I think I already know," I answered. "Is it…"

"Yep! It's a boy!"

Kim smirked as she hunted and pecked at the keyboard with her free hand. Seconds later, the words flashed onto the screen: "IT'S A BOY!!!!!!!!"

This particular boy was straddling the camera in a bawdy display of masculinity, but Kim added a vivid white arrow to remove any doubt.

I lifted my hands to my mouth and giggled, blinking back tears. The four of us fell into a clumsy group hug.

We're having a boy! The phrase flashed across my mind like a news headline, and I imagined God giving me a wink and a nudge. He truly was watching over every detail of this pregnancy, I marveled, and he cared about the desire Mark and I had deemed too bold to voice.

After the appointment, Mark and Steve headed back to work and Johnna and I back home. After schlepping through the door with my girls and their gear, I quickly dialed Grandma and Grandpa Westfield.

"I just wanted to call and tell you that we're having a boy," I announced, "and we're going to name him Mark Westfield."

There was silence on the other end of the line as the news sunk in, then a happy, "Oh, that's wonderful!" from my grandma.

Grandpa was quiet, but I could hear him breathing, perhaps gathering his thoughts.

"Thank you, Sarah," he drawled. And that was all.

Grandpa Westfield, like my Grandpa Sisson 12 years earlier, was battling cancer. The last few months had slowed him, both physically and mentally, and the man who had lived by the motto "If you rest, you rust" had started to surrender to cancer's imminent victory.

Grandpa felt secure in the legacy of his two daughters. Now the surname his father had carried from the Netherlands would carry on. Mark and I would call our baby "West" and even "Mark Westfield" to drive home a point. We were trying to honor my grandfather's memory and instill in our son a namesake of strength and purpose.

As the girls picked over their food around the dinner table that evening, Mark and I revealed the news. At three-and-a-half and 18 months, Lainey and Faith were curious if largely detached. Lainey's more pressing concern was whether she had eaten enough "real food" to qualify for dessert.

Mark posed an irresistible question to get the girls in the spirit.

"What do you think we should name the little guy?" he asked, eyebrows raised.

Faith, as always, deferred to her big sister. Still staring at the dreaded peas upon her plate, Lainey casually replied, "Cosmo."

My eyes met Mark's across the table. How had Lainey come up with this moniker from our favorite '90s sitcom? I could only conclude that our heavenly father, the one who delighted in us, cared as much about our laughter as our tears.

.

CHAPTER 22

False Alarms

*M*onths five, six, and seven marched on while Johnna and I scrapbooked, took in chick flicks, and stalked sales racks for maternity clothes. We'd made it to the third trimester, and I watched our baby's development closely via *What to Expect When You're Expecting*, a.k.a. the pregnant woman's bible. The book I once longed to burn for all the pain it caused me now sat on my nightstand for quick reference. Since the ultrasound, our 30-week-old baby had grown from the size of a medium banana to a three-pound, 18-inch, coughing, hiccupping, jabbing Muhammed Ali.

As Johnna's belly grew, we'd proudly introduced her to the rest of our tribe, including Mark's parents, who trekked north from Virginia over Thanksgiving. Finally, around Christmas, Reneé made the eight-hour trek from Iron Mountain in the U.P. to meet the woman who had offered up her womb for me. After hugs and tears and Reneé's hands traversing Johnna's bulging belly, my best friend declared, "I wish I could buy you a car!"

In early January—with our due date only six weeks out—I bathed nearly every waking and dreaming moment in prayer; nothing eloquent, only a constant turning to God to shoulder my unease as we crept toward "full-term." In Michigan, snow crouched on sidewalks and towered in grey buttes at the edges of store parking lots. Sheets of ice covered driveways and were by then impervious to salt.

One night, as I scraped uneaten spaghetti into the garbage and Mark wrestled with the girls on the floor, the phone rang. On the other end, Johnna was distraught.

"I fell," she cried. "I was just walking into the house, and I slipped."

"Are you OK?" I asked. I was afraid to hear the answer.

"I'm OK," Johnna replied. "I think he's OK. I fell on my knee…hard, but I don't think it hurt the baby. It just really scared me."

"I'll be right over."

I gave Mark a quick explanation and dashed out the door as fast as one can when snow boots, zippers, and winter accessories are involved. Johnna and Steve's house was only a five-minute drive from ours. When I burst through the Garretts' front door, I found Johnna on the couch, feet up on a stool, both hands planted on her belly.

"He's alright. He's moving," she assured me with a relieved smile.

I plopped down next to Johnna and stretched my fingers out on either side of hers, resting my head on her shoulder. We stayed that way for several minutes, feeling the baby's movement. The little dude seemed remarkably active for early evening. Johnna's fall had probably woken him up.

"I'm sorry I scared you," Johnna whispered hoarsely. "We're just so close and it freaked me out."

"It's OK," I said. "We're OK."

With the danger behind us, Johnna gave me the whole story, specifically the part about how she tried to "fall properly." I stifled a grin. If Johnna had fallen properly, she would've put out her hands to protect herself. Instead, she chose to protect her belly, but she would recover.

Johnna's instinct to protect and care for the little life she carried struck me. Some might chalk her efforts up to maternal instinct, and that was certainly part of it. But there was also the part wherein Johnna had adopted as her own my deepest longing for a baby.

As it turned out, Johnna's fall was not the biggest problem we faced in January. The county court date loomed for our pre-birth order approval. The judge had to sign the order before Johnna landed in the hospital in labor. Our lawyer had contacted us the week before with news: Our case had been assigned to the Honorable Judge Cornella, the most experienced (read: oldest) judge in the county.

Mark and I secretly hoped that our shared Italian roots would give us a leg-up with the aging judge and compel him to sign the order post-haste. All we had to do was show up and let Eric do his thing, and, at the end of the brief hearing, we would be legally cleared to take our little Rollandini home from the hospital.

On the day of our hearing, Mark and I donned our best "upstanding citizen" attire and walked respectfully into the old county court room. The room's mahogany panels gleamed, and the smell of Murphy's Oil Soap hung in the air. We took our seats in the front row. Eric stood at the podium and expounded on the logic and legality behind a pre-birth order.

Judge Cornella sat stoically at his bench, bespectacled face unreadable. Eric made the case with intelligence and conviction. Our pre-birth order hinged only on the technicality of a judge's John Hancock.

Unfortunately, Judge Cornella didn't see it that way. Southwest Michigan's small, conservative Allegan County court system had never seen a custodial rights case involving a gestational carrier, so the novelty of our request translated into a good deal of suspicion. At age 71, Judge Cornella had 35 years of experience in dressing down all but the most prepared attorneys. That day, the judge fixated on the issue of inheritance rights, which determine who can claim property after a death.

His honor's central question was this: Could a woman give birth to a baby and said baby *not* hold legal rights to some of that woman's (namely Johnna's) assets upon death? These inheritance rights had been on the books in every state in the country for eons. How could a new-fangled document called a pre-birth order do away with generations of precedent?

Mark and I watched the tennis match. The judge unleashed a barrage of questions, and Eric returned each volley. At the end of the match, the two had reached a stalemate, and Eric hustled us out of the courtroom and into an adjacent meeting room.

"What just happened?" Mark and I wondered.

Eric, who had handled similar cases all over Michigan, was perplexed but calm.

"The judge isn't going to sign the order today. He needs some time to think on it."

"How long does he need?" I asked. "The baby's due in four and a half weeks."

"I don't know—hopefully just a couple of days." Eric sounded far from certain.

"And what happens if he refuses to sign it?" Mark chimed in.

"Well, I believe he will sign it, but, if he doesn't, we'll have to do a home study and involve an outside agency to make it legal."

"Are you saying," I pressed, "that we're going to have to adopt our own baby?"

"I don't think it will come to that, but yes."

The Shower Sequel

The following weekend, Mom held a shower for baby number three. By this time, everyone within a country mile had heard about our unusual pregnancy and—like my parents nine months earlier—was dying to get a closer look at Johnna.

Many of these small-town folks had concerns, likely due to a recent Texas court case in which a gestational carrier had sued for custody after delivering the baby...and won. In fact, since we already had a house full of bottles, blankets, clothing, and baby miscellany, the purpose of the shower was to let normalcy take the edge off people's worry.

Along with Johnna and me, Mom had fielded countless awkward questions about the gestational carrier and considered the shower a way to offer honest answers straight from the horses' mouths. To this end, Johnna and I spent weeks before the party creating a list of questions people had asked about gestational surrogacy and the nature of our unique friendship, tummy mom and expectant mom.

The day of the shower, Johnna and I sat side by side amidst clucking of women young and old. Mom passed a basket full of question slips around the circle for each woman to take and read aloud. Questions like, *Won't your relationship be weird after the baby comes?* And for Johnna:

How do you know you're not going to want to keep the baby?

Johnna and I answered each question candidly while some guests plucked tissues from the circulating Kleenex box. After each answer, I opened the questioner's gift. Johnna declined to help with present opening, content to watch me tear into boxes and bags filled with every shade of blue. Some women had brought goodies like candles, lotions, and fuzzy socks for Johnna as well.

We nibbled chicken salad croissants and chocolate-dipped strawberries, flocking around a table of portraits that Johnna and I had taken weeks earlier when we marched into Target and declared, "Pose us!" The bubbly photographer had jumped into the unusual task with zeal, giving us a collection of photos featuring fingers curled around Johnna's belly, two faces beaming.

I watched women cross over from skeptics to believers that afternoon. My mom said later that the profound friendship that Johnna and I shared, along with our mutual love for this baby, had pierced through all the doubt about Johnna's motives and my naïveté.

Two weeks dragged on, and then a third, with no word from Judge Cornella. Mark and I called Eric daily to check in, but the answer was always, "Nothing yet." Since the baby was due in less than two weeks, Mark had started planning for the contingency of a new home study and private adoption, price tag $5,000–$10,000. I was beyond angry that we had jumped through hoop after hoop only to spend our family's money placating this dinosaur of a judge. Our only consolation was that Rollandini vs. Cornella might grease the skids for future couples walking through infertility.

On February 8, 2007, in our 39th week of pregnancy, Johnna and I walked in to see Dr. Menapace for her routine check-up. Well, I walked and Johnna wobbled. There was no seeing beyond her distended belly, so Johnna took each step with caution. She had begun experiencing Braxton Hicks contractions, the preliminary cramping of the uterus that's more uncomfortable than painful and more unpredictable than the timed contractions of true labor.

With Johnna situated in the waiting room, I headed back to the restroom. Johnna and I joked often about the sympathy symptoms that her pregnancy had triggered in me, including frequent trips to the ladies' room.

As I pushed the door open to the exam hallway, I spied a cluster of nurses chatting in hushed tones. Curious, I inched toward the bathroom, attempting to eavesdrop. Snippets of their discussion floated in the air. *Phone call, thirty-nine weeks, no movement, no heartbeat, delivered stillborn.*

My heart sped up, and dread lodged like a steel knot in my stomach. When I returned to the waiting room, I filled Johnna in on the conversation before a nurse called us back to see the doctor.

By the time we moved into the exam room, I was in full-fledged panic mode.

"How could that happen?" I asked Dr. Menapace when he arrived after the nurse's initial check. "How could a woman carry a healthy baby that far into a pregnancy only to have the baby die when it's just a few days from being born?"

Johnna—his prenatal patient—was fine, but it was clear to Dr. Menapace that I needed an intervention. The doctor parked himself on the stool and wheeled it over to me until we were knee-to-knee.

"First of all, take a deep breath and calm down," he ordered.

I did.

"I'm sorry you overheard that conversation. The nurses were talking about a patient in a different office."

I nodded my head, searching for comfort in the doctor's expertise.

"Sarah, I deliver hundreds of babies every year, and I only see a case like this once every few years."

"But what causes it?" I repeated.

Information was my only ally. Maybe the doctor could give me some facts to help me rule out a tragedy.

Now it was Dr. Menapace's turn to take a deep breath, likely mustering his patience.

"It's very rare, but sometimes a baby develops a knot in its cord, which tightens in the final weeks of pregnancy, interfering with blood circulation and cutting off the baby's oxygen."

I concentrated on breathing deeply. I wished for a window into Johnna's uterus, but all I had were her kick counts.

Dr. Menapace put both hands on my shoulders, forcing me to meet his gaze.

"That is not going to happen to your baby. You'll be holding this little guy before you know it."

The hourly prayers that had grounded me for the last nine months now filled every remaining crevice of time. I chanted Romans 8:28 as I scrambled for peace: *God is working for my good.* In the week leading up to our due date, this total reliance on the Lord's steadfast trustworthiness kept me from constant despair and probably helped stave off a psychotic break.

February marked the 10-year anniversary of that momentous weekend when Mark and I naïvely endeavored to get pregnant on our very first try. Even with Johnna's behemoth belly and the baby's kick-boxing, I found it difficult to believe that Mark and I would soon snuggle our son and trace his features back up the Sisson and Rollandini family trees.

Two days after our unnerving appointment with Doctor Menapace, Johnna and I sped to the hospital with a promise to call our husbands if we needed them.

Since Johnna's previous deliveries had involved only minutes of pushing, Dr. Menapace advised heading to the hospital at the first signs of labor. Getting Johnna to full term had taken a great deal of manpower and a fortune in medical care. Nobody wanted this baby to be born at home, or, worse, in the car on the way to the hospital.

The nurses hooked Johnna up to a fetal monitor and checked her progress for an hour before they unhooked her and encouraged us to take a lap around the obstetrics wing. As we shuffled our way past rooms—some with women in labor, others filled with balloons and nursing babies—I willed our baby to begin his descent through the birth canal.

"Do you think it's working?" I asked Johnna.

She looked miserable.

"I don't know. I think my contractions have stopped."

"You know, my mother-in-law was an OB nurse for thirty years. She says hospitals should put tracks with lane markers on the delivery floors for all the expectant moms who walk to get their babies to cooperate."

Johnna laughed. "Does the walking help?"

I put my arm around Johnna's waist to steady her, wishing I could give a different answer.

"She didn't seem to think it did much to speed up labor, but it gives women something to do besides just lie there and wait."

When we returned to our room, the nurses noted that Johnna's contractions had stopped. It was time to chalk up our visit to a false alarm. Poor Johnna. She was in her last days of pregnancy and had all the annoying symptoms to prove it. Lugging around an extra 30 pounds made her constantly tired, and she had trouble catching her breath. Her back ached. Her heartburn roared. Finding a comfortable sleeping position was impossible. She visited the bathroom with the frequency of a commuter train at Grand Central Station. To top off this mixed bag of maladies, her ankles and legs had swollen like sausages. And Johnna endured all of it agreeably for me.

We were in the home stretch, yet the finale felt miles away. Johnna and I were both ready for the fat lady to sing already. Like Reneè, I would have loved to purchase Johnna a shiny new Maserati in return for her service—heck, in my estimation, even a luxury beach house in Key West would constitute underappreciation. In the end, though, all I could offer Johnna was a six-week membership to Nurtisystem to burn off her baby weight, along with a lifetime of family snapshots that included a boy who I hoped would be the spitting image of his dad.

CHAPTER 23

Grand Finale

*I*t was February 14, and we sat around our dinner table with the girls eating red Jell-O and heart-shaped pancakes, sipping from fancy glasses of sparkling cran-apple juice. Our Valentine's tradition revolved around each one of us sharing what we loved about the others while scarfing down breakfast for dinner.

After Faith doled out applesauce kisses, Lainey dove into her fondness for wrestling with Daddy and bedtime reading with Mama. She babbled on about how much she "wuved" our pets as her sticky fingers reached under the table to grab Giuseppe's wiry fur. The phone rang. *Probably a telemarketer,* I thought, miffed at the lack of reverence for family time.

"Hello?"

"Hi Sarah—it's Eric Phillips."

"Oh, sorry! Hi!" I quickly walked back the annoyance in my voice.

"I just wanted to call to give you the good news," Eric continued. "Judge Cornella signed the order."

Eric's voice resounded with the thrill of victory and I shouted out the news.

Mark scooped up the girls and promenaded around our table.

"Thanks, Eric! So what happens now?"

"I'll overnight the order to the hospital. When Johnna goes into labor, you'll be good to go!"

Relief washed over me. The pre-birth order was one detail that—until now—had failed to fall into place. I'd even asked my cousin David, a local lawyer, to address the judge's misgivings over lunch, but Judge Cornella hadn't budged. It had been over a month since our hearing and, with four days left until our due date, Mark and I had given up on the judge's signature.

What had made him finally see the light? Like so many questions, I'd never learn the answer.

But here we were—all ready for the big day—and Mark and I didn't even have to smuggle our baby home from the hospital in lieu of a $7,000 adoption fee. Happy Valentine's Day to us!

Go Time

Two days later, Johnna called at 5 a.m. Contractions demanded that Steve get her to the hospital.

Johnna and I had gone to a check-up the day before, and, still three days away from her due date, she had begged Dr. Menapace to strip her membranes. The doctor had acquiesced and used a gloved finger to gently separate the amniotic sac from the wall of the uterus. Although the procedure, which can release hormones that trigger contractions, has mixed results, in Johnna's case, it had worked. Less than 12 hours after her appointment, our baby was in pole position.

Mark and I gave our sleeping girls a little peck as we made our way out the door and thanked our neighbor for stepping in. We hoped this wasn't another false start.

Dr. Menapace was hemming and hawing about whether he would keep Johnna in the hospital when Mark and I barged in. The doctor jabbed his thumb in my direction.

"This one's too high strung. I think we better get this baby out today so she can stop worrying."

I threw my arms around Dr. Menapace and thanked him then turned my attention to Johnna.

"How are you feeling?"

"Ready!" she groaned.

Her face was flushed, but she was beaming, relieved at the prospect of getting her body—and her life—back in a matter of hours.

We followed behind the nurses as they wheeled Johnna into the birthing room, and I thought about how different this hospital experience would be compared to Lainey's and Faith's births.

Our two adoptions had worked out perfectly, but the hours we spent waiting for our girls were dampened by the awareness that they weren't ours yet and—short the iron will of their birth mothers—might never be. I had been a bystander at Nita's and Amy's bedsides, preparing myself for the worst-case scenario: leaving the hospital without a baby.

In contrast, I had invested my whole self in the mothering that waited at the end of Johnna's labor. Amidst all my doubting, I'd never questioned her sincerity or her conviction that this baby was ours. Johnna had allowed me to drop my wall of self-protection and embrace my baby with an unchecked love from minute one.

Even so, as we watched Johnna's labor progress, I continued to expect someone in authority to burst in and say, "Just joking! She's not really in labor. Go home. Better luck next time!" But the labor graph continued to document the rising peaks of Johnna's contractions.

Surprisingly, she was in high spirits. So much so that I found it hard to believe she was inching toward delivery.

Then I had a realization. Nita had waited too long to ask for an epidural. Amy's preeclampsia made pain relief impossible. Johnna, however, happily said yes to the cocktail of anesthesia and opioids. We two couples were thus empowered to watch TV, chat with friends who popped in, and generally carry on like we were hosting a small Super Bowl party.

Johnna held court from her propped-up hospital bed while our husbands discussed Steve's ambition to hike the Appalachian Trail. Johnna had promised him time off to hit the trail in return for his support of her dream. As I studied Steve's mellow steadiness, I thanked God for his generosity.

Our afternoon fiesta turned into more of a business meeting when Johnna wobbled out of the bathroom and announced, "My water broke," before climbing back into bed.

I had somehow missed this milestone with Nita and Amy and had expected it to be followed by screaming. I mean the big screen always followed water-breaking with an insane brouhaha.

Ha! No sending us home now! I thought.

Mom, Dad, Craiger, and eight-year-old Maddy camped out in the waiting room. When it came time for Johnna to push at around 4:30 p.m., I sprinted down to let them know Baby Rollandini was on the way. It was the first time we'd had our own welcoming committee at the hospital.

The gray winter light that seeped in through the hospital window drained into dusk, and I had nothing on my mental docket but getting Johnna to 10 centimeters. I wiped clammy palms on my pants before clamping down Johnna's hand. Mark stood beside me.

That we were mere moments away from our baby's birth felt impossible. Even now, I couldn't imagine seeing his face. In a flash, 10 years of questions I hadn't dared ask tumbled into my mind. Would our baby have hair? Would his face be round or long and narrow? Would his belly button be an innie or an outie?

Meanwhile, Johnna closed her eyes through each contraction. I watched her deliver grimace after grimace and wished we had planned out our *modus operandi* for the actual labor. Egg retrieval, embryo transfer, and nine months of pregnancy cravings done together, I was buffaloed by the question of what I could do to help her at game time. Should I adopt the role of enthusiastic cheerleader or gentle counselor? I shot for a happy medium. If I had been in Johnna's place, I would've ordered the whole room to shut up and leave me alone.

When the doctor-on-call whisked in, I knew we were getting close. The physician wore a messy blond ponytail and looked like one of my high school students. She wheeled over a small stool and checked Johnna's progress then strapped on a plastic face shield. She seemed more prepared for a welding job than to deliver an infant.

"OK, Johnna, let's push now," she ordered. "The baby's ready."

Mark, Steve, and I took the cue for encouraging words.

"You're doing great. We're almost there."

I pulled Mark up to my position and put Johnna's hand in his so I could get a first glimpse of our son.

His rounded head, covered in black hair, slowly emerged from the birth canal. For a split second, I was stunned. *That's our baby's head.* The doctor cradled his head and neck with both hands as the rest of his gangly body made its way into the room.

His shivering wail complemented the smell of blood and disinfectant.

As the doctor reached to snip the umbilical cord, the nurse announced, "Look at this! We've got a miracle baby: he has a knot in his cord!"

The nurse's words jolted me and my eyes met Johnna's. I wrapped my arms around her and we bawled together. *Our baby had a knot in his cord.*

Since that morning, the hospital staff had dubbed our little guy a miracle because of the reproductive technology and altruism that had made Johnna's pregnancy possible. But because of our conversation with Dr. Menapace less than a week ago, Johnna and I grasped full well the miracle the nurse now cradled. Our boy had been born with a tangled lifeline, one that should've stopped his heart. Instead, somehow the coil held just enough slack to deliver him to us unharmed.

The doctor glanced up at us. "He truly is a miracle baby," she whispered.

God's presence was palpable. More than spirit, his power loomed like another person standing at Johnna's bedside. In those moments, confidence replaced my doubt. *For this child I prayed.*

"Thank you," I blubbered to Johnna, knowing the phrase was a rickety bridge to span a chasm of gratitude.

I plunged into Mark's arms.

"He's here," Mark murmured into my hair.

"Yes," I cried. "Finally."

I reached for the wad of tissue in my pocket. "Let's go see him!" I pleaded.

Mark laughed and led me to the other side of the curtain, where a nurse was working on our son. Perched above the bassinet, I scrutinized every inch of him, searching for a defect that could snatch away the wonder.

I found only a perfectly formed little boy, a carbon copy of his daddy, but so much more the workmanship of God.

I reached down and stroked his palm until his long fingers latched on to mine.

"Nine pounds, four ounces, and 20 and a half inches long!" the nurse said. "His head is 36 centimeters. Way to go, Johnna!"

From the other side of the curtain, we heard her chuckle.

"I told you his head was big!"

The nurse marveled as she flipped him back and forth.

"He looks like he's a month old. We're going to call him Bubba!"

I jetted out to the waiting room to give Bubba's fan club the news.

When I returned, Mark held a swaddled and be-hatted Mark Westfield, identical noses brushing in an Eskimo kiss.

"My turn!" I said.

Mark handed over our baby, and I felt his compact weight in the crook of my arms. The receiving blanket and knit beanie covered all but his face and drew attention to wide-set blue eyes and wispy eyebrows punctuating the disgruntled expression of an old man. *I might never look away.*

The sound of the curtain being yanked open reminded me there was someone else who would appreciate seeing "Bubba." I strolled over to Johnna and laid West in her arms.

"He's perfect," I said softly, sitting down on the edge of her bed.

"He sure is…except that he looks just like Mark!"

My husband was uncharacteristically speechless.

We sat there in silence for a few minutes exploring West's face with the fading sense that all was right with the world.

"OK, I'm starving," Johnna declared, handing West back to me, and, in a rare show of bossiness, she bellowed, "Bring me some dinner!"

While Johnna waited for her dinner tray, she had a phone call to make. Her son, Zach, was celebrating his birthday without her. She just happened to have been in the hospital in a similar position on this day nine years earlier.

Mom, Dad, Craiger, and Maddy joined the party, and Maddy alone remained unmoved by a cousin who bore a strong resemblance to Ebenezer Scrooge. What was the big deal?

Mom grabbed her camera and snapped enough pictures to make up for the ones she'd missed with our girls' births. I could almost see Dad daydreaming about John Deere, baseball mitts, and mud-covered overalls. Along with the other 300,000 families across the globe who welcomed babies that day, we pondered the potential of this life, but we probably spent a bit more time than most considering the past, the season of winter we had all trudged through to arrive here.

"He's beautiful, isn't he?" Johnna asked, scarfing down turkey and gravy. My parents grinned.

"But when we all get home," Johnna continued, "*I* will be sleeping all night and Mark and Sarah will be up feeding West!" She giggled before stabbing another green bean.

Johnna was putting everyone at ease again. She was no maniacal surrogate mother planning to snatch the baby. Her logic-defying love had unraveled everyone's cynicism and piqued my desire to trust God more intentionally. If the creator of the universe still prompted extraordinary action from not just the Mother Teresas and Bill Grahams of the world but from everyday saints like Johnna, it was time for me to press in closer to discern his cues in my life.

Homecoming

When we arrived home the next morning, Mom and Dad were waiting for us, along with Lainey and Faith, all shined up with dresses and bows. The girls took turns holding "Baby West" on our couch. The Garrett clan joined us later to heighten the celebration while neighbors and family streamed in and out all day. Exhausted and overwhelmed, I was ready to kick out the party guests and get back to normal, however "normal" would look with three kiddos under age four.

Holding Lainey in my lap while others passed West around, I suddenly realized how warm her little body felt against mine. I snagged the digital thermometer, which reported her temperature as 104 degrees. Her heart was moving so rapidly that I couldn't track the beats.

No God, I pleaded. *You can't give me a son only to take away my daughter.*

My rash thinking highlighted my volatile faith. After four years of miracles, I had come to anticipate tragedy.

Of course, Lainey fell sick on a Saturday, so we had to trek back to the hospital we just left instead of visiting the pediatrician.

In the waiting room, I rocked her back and forth, continuing my decade-long dialogue with God, which had never paused long enough for an "amen."

Be with my baby girl. Help the doctors figure out what's wrong with her. Keep her safe. I love her so much. Lord, please don't take her from me.

In other words, *God, don't mess with my kids.* This is every mother's selfish prayer. We forget that our children first belong to God, who is not just loving but love itself. And we imagine that we could love our children more than the God who knitted them together.

I'd taken Lainey to the hospital with strep and arrived home with amoxicillin. Placing her gently into her bed, I kissed her forehead.

Thank you, God, for the medicine that soothes my firstborn and will see her dancing again in a few days.

Then I made my way from room to room in the hushed stillness. Across the hall in a big-girl bed, I kneeled next to Faith. I admired her petite features, so contrary to her larger-than-life personality and stubborn nature.

Thank you for sticking with me in my doubt, Lord, for making this strong little girl mine.

Padding through the kitchen to our bedroom, I found Mark sound asleep and West stirring in the bassinet beside him. I lifted my not-quite-two-day-old to my chest and swayed, glancing between Mark's slumbering form and West's.

Thank you, Father, for this little guy and the big one sleeping over there. I'm sorry I still spend so much time doubting when you have been consistently faithful.

I carried West into the kitchen to fix a bottle, a tricky one-handed operation I had mastered years earlier, and plopped down in the living room chair. As I rocked my son, I breathed in the smell of baby skin and formula. I drank in his fresh face, carving West's features into my heart alongside those of my steadfast husband and two little girls. God had chosen these faces for me, each one irreplaceable in his sovereign design.

The scuff-scuff of little feet in footie pajamas ended my reflection.

"Hi, Mama! I missed you," exclaimed Faithy as she clambered onto my lap.

I pulled her closer. "I missed you too, Munchkin."

"Where's Lala?"

"She's tired, honey. Do you think we can be extra quiet so Lala can sleep? We want her to feel better."

Faith, ever the helper, pressed finger to lips.

"Shhhh. I can be quiet!"

I gave her a smiling nod of approval.

We snuggled while she pointed at her brother's face and proudly named each of its parts. *Eyes. Nose. Mouth. Ears.*

Tiring of the game, she glanced up at me and flashed an impish grin. "Oatmeal?"

"It *is* time for breakfast, isn't it?"

Faith nodded, pleased that Mommy had caught on so quickly.

"Yes, let's go get you something to eat."

This was my life now. The life of a young mom. Reverent awe mixed with oatmeal and spit up. Only I wasn't so young, nearly 37 actually.

If my plan of long ago had gone off without a hitch, our house would've been filled with kids half grown by this time. And I would've missed out on getting to know the God I professed to follow. He was a God with hard edges, his will not easily explained away by Christian clichés. Even as I sat with my blessings, the awareness of still-waiting friends stirred a familiar restlessness. My friend Kelly had given birth to two children who died within hours of delivery. My co-worker Melissa and her husband had spent thousands on treatment but were still childless. Patty and Mike brought a baby home only for the birth mom to change her mind a day before the court hearing. How could God reshape these heartaches into something good?

His provision for Mark and me had caused me to abide in his promises. A genuine new hope dwelled within me; however, my wrestling spirit refused to forfeit my own will—my questions—without a fight. Even though my belief often felt like shifting sand, in 10 years of infertility, faith had become the daily choice that saved me.

ACKNOWLEDGMENTS

The task of thanking everyone who has had a part in helping me finish this book feels quite overwhelming. If I've left someone out, please blame it on my addled brain, largely absorbed in the challenges of parenting teenagers.

Many, many thanks to my brilliant and patient editor, Jess Andrews; working with you has been like earning a PhD in literary prose. Thankfully, you have my undying gratitude because you certainly didn't get paid enough to do the job!

I appreciate the friends I've met at Write to Publish, Tracy Nielsen, Beth Ziarnik, John Turney, Kristine Orkin, Tonia Woolever, Cynthia Ruchti, Jane Rubietta, Candice James, Lin Johnson, Kathy Carlton Willis, and Cyle Young. Thank you for the late-night chats and critiques in the dorm lobby at Wheaton College. Your encouragement, prayers, and belief in me have spurred me on to the finish line!

My social media sisters have transformed this introvert into a believer in the power of online connections. Thank you Melanie Redd, Dawn Klinge, Bethany Kimsey, Melanie Kendall, Betsy Pendergrass, Janelle Esker, Cindy LaFavre Yorks, Jane Delong, Tina Smith, Nina Blevins, Marva Smith, Laura Thomas, Angela Lawley, Amy Hamilton, Kirsty Maginness, Shilah Goin, Brittany Bonnaffons, Dominique Young, Dianne Thornton, Ruthie Gray, Sandra Bretschneider, Helen Jamieson, April Swiger, Laura Corbin, Pam and Ayanna. Your everyday wisdom and faith in Jesus have given me the strength and motivation to stay true to my God-given message.

I'm grateful for my writing girlfriends, Tish Suk, Casey Bender-Butler, Ronnell Gibson, Lisa McEachin, Heather Kaufman, and Heather Roberts.

You have taught me so much about friendship and accountability. Can't wait for our next girls' weekend. No tow truck necessary, I promise!

Big hugs to the TTC friends who have consistently shared their stories with me, including Jay and Becci, Scott and Amy, Cletus and Kari, Brian and Kristin, Tony and Stacy, Ryan and Ashley, Ryan and Mary, as well as Sarah and little Maxwell. Your vulnerability has informed my writing. Thank you for educating me with your unique perspectives.

Carol Kent and Carla Gasser, your writing and speaking ministries along with your authentic faith inspire me daily. Thank you for lifting me up and challenging me to offer my best to readers.

My students at Wayland Union High School have enthusiastically supported my platform-building efforts and devotedly listened to parts of this book for many years. I love you guys.

So much love for these in-real-life friends, Renee'Yake, Diane Williams, Gina Watson, Diane Glessner, Ann Woudwyk, Tami Hjelm, Bev Rearick, Amy Huyck, Tessa Potgeter, Becky Black, Andrea Brown, Caitlin Moritz, Rochelle Diaz, Amy Nelson, Kim Carter, Sharon Doelker, Ace Hulbert and Carter and Betsy Lezman. You've never stopped asking, "So when's your book coming out?" You've helped me to believe that my writing matters.

Drs. Dodds and Young at The Fertility Center in Grand Rapids, Michigan; you carried my dream of having a family for as many years as I did. Thank you for your expertise and your compassionate bedside manner.

Carol the perky receptionist, Shelly Nibbelink, and Michelle Dykema at Adoption Associates, your love for all members of the adoption triad as well as your passion for building families through adoption inspire countless birth families and waiting couples. Thank you for your part in making us parents of two precious daughters.

Amy and Nita, thank you for choosing adoption. Your courage and selflessness are unrivaled. There are no words for the lifetime of gratitude you've instilled in Mark and me. Our daughters remind us of each of you in so many ways; their lives propel us toward praising our God of the impossible!

Johnna Garrett, you are crazy, girl! You actually listen for the Lord's voice and follow his prompting. I can only imagine what this world would look like if more believers did the same. You've given us a son to round out our family and we've given you stretch marks. Best deal ever! Seriously, thank you, my dear friend.

Steve, Cassidy, and Zach, thanks for sharing her! I know it wasn't always easy.

I have so much supportive family, it doesn't seem fair. Thanks and love to the Rollandini clan who checked in regularly on my book progress, including Herman and Martha, Carla, Marcee, Cathy, Joyce, Andrea, Jacqui, and Laura.

I appreciate the Westfield and Sisson gangs, whose members have enthusiastically supported my writing ministry since its inception—hugs and appreciation to my grandparents in heaven, Red and Ellen Sisson and Fred and Donna Westfield, as well as to my mom and dad, Stephen, Abby, and Maddy Sisson, Judy Kiel, Barb Sisson, Barb Jirgens, and Chris McNutt, and the many cousins who I am honored to call family.

And finally, to my favorite people in the entire world... I thank God every day for the blessing of living life with you, Mark. You've supported my writing both physically and financially and loved me through the toughest 10 years of our lives. Thank you for saying yes even when your first inclination was "Heck no!" You give me balance and make our lives an adventure. Love you, Shmoopie!

To Adelaine, Faith, and West, your faces are like oxygen to me. Loving you well is my first and last purpose. Thank you for giving me uninterrupted time (ha!) to write. I pray that this book fills you with the certainty that God is the author of your stories and that he will continue to guide your lives with kindness and purpose.

Self-Publishing School

NOW IT'S YOUR TURN

Discover the EXACT 3-step blueprint you need to become a bestselling author in as little as three months.

Self-Publishing School helped me, and now I want them to help you with this FREE resource to begin outlining your book!

Even if you're busy, bad at writing, or don't know where to start, you CAN write a bestseller and build your best life.

With tools and experience across a variety of niches and professions, Self-Publishing School is the <u>only</u> resource you need to take your book to the finish line!

DON'T WAIT

Say "YES" to becoming a bestseller:

https://self-publishingschool.com/friend/

Follow the steps on the page to get a FREE resource to get started on your book and unlock a discount to get started with Self-Publishing School.

ABOUT THE AUTHOR

*S*arah and her husband, Mark, endured a decade of infertility to finally build their family through domestic adoption and gestational surrogacy. Sarah is an author, a worship leader, and an American Sign Language teacher at a public high school, striving to shine the light of Christ in all of the dark places. On any given day, you might find Sarah walking her three rescue mutts, forcing her family into a board game challenge, or plumbing the profound insights found in Dove dark chocolate wrappers.

She is the creator of *Infertility Club*, a Midwest ministry for women struggling with infertility. You can read her work in *The Penasee Globe*, *christiandevotions.us*, *Focus on the Family magazine*, and *Unlocked: Devotions for Teens*. A part of her story is also featured in the book *Staying Power: Building a Stronger Marriage When Life Sends Its Worst*. She blogs at *Real Life, Real Faith*.

Sarah's greatest hope is to be an encourager of others who find themselves asking tough questions in the middle of real life. A portion of the sales from her book, *Life after Infertility*, will support Focus on the Family's *Option Ultrasound*, which provides grants for ultrasound machines and sonography training for crisis pregnancy clinics in high-abortion communities. Sarah lives near Grand Rapids, Michigan with her husband, their three children, and frequent exchange students. Learn more by visiting www.sarahrollandini.com.

Can You Help?

Thank You for Reading My Book!

I really appreciate all of your feedback, and
I love hearing what you have to say.

I need your input to make the next version of
this book and my future books better.

Please leave me an honest review on Amazon letting me
know what you thought of *Life After Infertility*.

Thanks so much!

Sarah

Made in the USA
Middletown, DE
25 May 2022

66166879R00135